UNLEASHING
THE
GOOD

UNLEASHING THE GOOD

How We Learn to Prioritize
The Common Good Over Personal Gain

TAISHA LALANAI RUCKER

ONE HUMANITY
PRESS

ONE HUMANITY
PRESS

To all who love and serve humanity.
May you stand together as a beacon of light in the
world, inspiring and drawing others seeking to shoulder
responsibility in service to the Common Good.

TABLE OF CONTENTS

MANTRAM FOR THE COMMON GOOD

Let us trust in the Good,
work for the Good,
live for the Good, and
will the Good for the Common Good

INTRODUCTION

THE OPTIMIST LOOKS around them, seeing only the good, true, and the beautiful despite appearances to the contrary. The realist purports to see things as they are despite evidence, however subtle, of what could be. To be an optimistic realist is to develop the capacity to look at people, circumstances, and the world at any point in time as a dual manifestation of what *is* and what *can be*. We are each a living, dynamic and ever-evolving life within the greater planetary Life, which is Itself *Becoming*. Just as human beings seek to organize and direct life to achieve their goals with greater or lesser success, this greater Life is in the process of organizing the many lives on this planet according to Its Will and Purpose to manifest the Good, True, and Beautiful for the benefit of all. However, presently, Earth's human kingdom, the mediator between the higher spiritual kingdoms and lower nonhuman kingdoms, and having "free will" rebels.

Instead of conforming to the Will of God, uniting all life in perfect harmony for the good of all, humanity instead chooses separateness, selfishness, and hatred, each of which blocks *the Good*.

Unleashing the Good: How We Learn to Prioritize the Common Good Over Personal Gain helps us begin where we are amidst unsettling and tectonic shifts affecting us personally, nationally, and worldwide to become channels for *the Good*. We can begin by acknowledging that national and world problems are a result of past errors and mistakes of humanity as a whole, that all problems can be solved when approached in a spirit of shared responsibility and cooperation rather than shaming and blaming, and that there is no part of the planetary body, including the human kingdom and its individual units, to which *the Good* does not flow absent its interruption, deflection, misuse, and misapplication. Right relations and goodwill, when practiced, solve all problems, restore the divine circulatory flow throughout the planet, and make humanity what it is — a divine center within the planetary body, illuminated from above and casting light and love to what is below.

Common good leaders are practical idealists. They glimpse, however faintly, new possibilities for world betterment. They are neither glamoured nor deceived by proffered solutions to humanity's problems that further divide and tether us to our past. Their focus is on building a brighter future for all. Contact with *the Good* and love for humanity inspires their thoughts and directs their activities. They aim to create structures supporting a new world culture based on sharing and cooperation.

We are living in a world created by humanity's collective and largely selfish ambitions and aspirations. As citizens of the wealthiest nation the world has ever known, Americans have an outsized impact and (I believe) an equivalent responsibility to help remake the world for the better. We can begin by changing our leadership paradigm to reward selflessness and cooperation. When leaders across public, private, and social institutions begin to set aside personal gain to achieve a common good, such leaders will help rebuild and restore faith in our institutions, heralding new possibilities for people and nations to join together to create a more interconnected and harmonious world – a world united by our shared pursuit of a better future for individuals, nations, and the planet we share.

1.

AMERICAN INDIVIDUALISM

AMERICAN, OR SO-CALLED rugged individualism, construed as independence, autonomy, and personal freedom, often persists at the expense of sharing, cooperation, and community. Describing someone as individualistic is a put-down. This label implies that we view such people as untrustworthy, selfish, and willing to prioritize their needs and desires above our own or others. Individualistic people take what they want, often demonstrating little to no concern for how what they want intersects with and impacts others' desires and needs. Similarly, individualistic corporations may prioritize shareholder and executive earnings over labor, environment, and community interests just as nations, under the banner of nationalism and imperialism, extract planetary resources without either equitable sharing or responsible restoration. Instead, nations, individually focused, conquer, expand, and hoard planetary resources to shore up wealth and power. Rugged individualism entrenches a winner-takes-all approach to life, relationships, business, and international diplomacy. Yet individuality is a necessary stage in the process of human development. In its true sense, becoming an individual or personality is the first paramount stage through which we extricate ourselves from the mass consciousness and become fully self-conscious, indicating a coordinated ability to impact our environment and recognize its impact upon us.

Individuality distinguishes humans from animals but only becomes fully operational when repurposed to thwart the baser selfish human instincts and express our potential for group consciousness and selflessness. In other words, when individuals see themselves as a whole in and of themselves rather than an integral part of the greater whole, which is the one humanity and the one planet, they falsely regard themselves as capable of survival independent of the larger universe to which they belong. More importantly, lacking awareness of their part in a larger whole, the rugged individualist is convinced that they can exist independent of the planetary life in which *we live and move and have our being*, ignorant of all that they receive from the natural world and others, justifying (in their minds) their refusal to give and shoulder appropriate responsibility.

Much of the modern world's economic, technological, and social achievements owe to the many named and unnamed driven personalities whose courage, tenacity, organization, and vision inspired global changes in how we work and live. Today, we need a new type of leader to carry forward a vision that builds a new and better world atop our rapidly decaying one, maintaining all that is good while transforming the dross of waning ideologies, institutions, and systems to serve the common good. The common good is not a socialist creed, as some would have us believe. It is simply a universal awareness of the interrelatedness between and among all living things — people and the planet — that engenders a growing sense of responsibility and a corresponding willingness to sacrifice for the good of the whole when this relatedness dawns upon our minds.

Years ago, working among diversity, equity, and inclusion practitioners, I became familiar with the term "whiteness." When used to describe a socio-political ideology, "whiteness" has historically acted as a substitute for the type of individualism we commonly understand as rugged individualism. Conflating rugged individualism and "whiteness" is erroneous, as there are people of every race, class, and nation who, at one time or another, have exhibited selfish individualism. Selfishness and separateness are shared human tendencies until we correctly orient ourselves to group recognition, group work, group service, and group good. To do so, we must strive to locate ourselves on the continuum between expressing our more self-centered desires and aspirations and a willingness to sacrifice these to benefit the common *Good*.

Many lists are circulating of characteristics of "white supremacy culture" or "whiteness," which include perfectionism or believing that there is one right way, urgency (moving too fast to include other voices, other ways of being), objectivity, the written word, individualism (rejecting the essentialness of our interdependence, etc.). As descriptors of so-called whiteness, these qualities converge at the most negative end of the individualism spectrum. They aptly describe a person and nation intent on preserving itself instead of the common good. By using "whiteness" instead of the more definite and appropriate term, *individualistic* or rugged individualism, is to ignore that developing an individualized consciousness (no longer "the sheep" of the human family) is a critical stage through which all people must pass to recognize and express their highest capacities, and to retard large-scale constructive personality development, a prerequisite for responsible national and global citizenship. Contributing to the common good implies self-awareness, self-determination, and self-expression adequate to benefit oneself and others, and are the fundamental aspects of selfhood.

Further, we can repurpose the ambition, hustle, and drive used to fulfill individual desires and goals through a correct orientation to the whole. To adequately contribute the best of who we are to our families, communities, nation, and world, we must first become a self, possessing the qualities that allow us to think for ourselves, undertake actions that align with our conscience, and become a force — for good or ill — in the world. Yet, when guided by a vision of the common good, we can become an individual equally aware of our capabilities and *responsibilities*. Rugged individualism may still exist as a brief stage in human development similar to the "terrible twos," in which toddlers challenge authority, vacillate from one mood to another, and throw tantrums when they don't get their way. But its wise handling will permit the natural maturation processes to lead humanity from a selfish to a more selfless individualism that supports cooperative living.

From an early age, I valued my independence, willingness to shoulder responsibility for myself and others, and an unequivocal reliance upon the voice within as the ultimate arbiter of my choices and decisions. This same individualism, of course, also sometimes made me difficult to deal with. My truth was *the truth*, my way was often *the way*, and I had (per my best friend) "emotions from a law book," making concern for how others thought and felt of negligible importance to me. Since you're already thinking about it, I'll say it. Some people accused me of having internalized "whiteness," which I quickly rejected. According to the "whiteness" doctrine, the rejection itself indicates a practice of white denial and characteristic defensiveness when accused of benefiting from our nation's racial caste system. Rejecting the label "whiteness" suggests an unwill-ingness to recognize how our socioeconomic-political systems legitimize some ways of being (mischaracterized as "whiteness") while invalidating others. Seeing myself clearly, I refused to blame white culture for qualities that I, as a black woman, felt were intrin-sically my own and had proven valuable when directed not so much to get what I wanted but to serve others. In other words, becoming a personality brought out the best in me even when, as it sometimes was, used selfishly. And I had the good sense to recognize that this was not a white people problem but a world culture problem. In every nation and among all classes, ethnicities, and religions, there are doggedly individual and inherently powerful people who have subverted responsibility even as they have become more capable. At times, I have been one of them. And I'm not alone.

When we recognize that what we've called "whiteness" is simply an *individualistic* or rugged individualism that must give way to a more enlightened individualism that develops each person's high-est potential in service to the common good, we can draw new lines and cast new affinities. Instead of the black-white divide, we will become a nation of two selves, one *selfish* and grasping, the other *selfless* and giving. Instead of arbitrary lines enforced by gated com-munities, divisive rhetoric, political maneuvering, and the many ways we individually and collectively game the system to get ahead, a new and fundamental affinity will form. Unlike present boundaries that preserve and exacerbate economic inequality, separate us along capricious lines of identities, and trap us in cycles of increasing par-tisanship, social distrust, and lack of faith in our institutions, we will recognize and lift up the strivers seeking to benefit the common good and that *Good* will necessarily include all, even the still self-serving other selves that make America what it is: a work in progress.

We need only look around at the many non-white people

choosing personal gain over the common good to recognize the universality of this aspect of our human condition. It would be helpful to the work that lay ahead if we substitute "individualistic" for "whiteness" and use instead "individualistic supremacy" over "white supremacy," understanding that had history swayed in another direction, the rugged individualism that prevents us from recognizing that we are individual parts of a greater whole could easily have had differently colored faces as its poster child. A supremacist culture constructs artificial hierarchies based on an arbitrary yet easily observable characteristic (skin color, ethnicity, nationality, social mores, gender, etc.) to create division, justifying the elevation of some and subjugation of others. Left unchecked, the divide between those who win and those who lose deepens, leaving only the most selfish people united against the common good.

In today's America, we cannot rely on political, economic, or social identities to determine on which side of history we stand, but whether we choose the common good over and above personal gain. Our nation isn't, in reality, divided between black-white, Muslim-Christian, wealthy-poor, college educated-non college-educated, suburban-city, owners-workers, Republican-Democrat, patriots-immigrants or any other characterization of Us versus Them. We are divided as people and nations between those determinedly selfish and those straining, however imperfectly, to create a harmonious world created by the best of us to bring out the best in us. We must discern among us who the selfless people are irrespective of their race, class, religion, political party, educational level, and likes and dislikes. We must strive to see with clarity those business executives, religious leaders, politicians, educators, filmmakers, artists, and decision-makers across all industries promoting a collective consciousness and shared vision of the good we can do when we direct our attention and efforts towards unleashing *the Good.*

Only the focused, directed public *will,* united in service to the whole, has the strength to fully eradicate a supremacist ideology, whether based on race, education, class, religion, politics, or another metric, because only recognition and responsible participation of each of us to achieve the common good validates our one humanity. It is time now that we reorient individualism from selfish use for personal gain to selfless service for the common good. When we couple the fearless independence gained through personal striving that rewards us with new capacities, broad contacts, and heightened vision with a selfless dedication to the common good, we embody a more enlightened individualism that can build a better world for all.

2.

OUR BETTER ANGELS

IN HIS FIRST inaugural address, President Abraham Lincoln called upon "The better angels of our nature" to address the deep divisions and tensions that were escalating between the Northern and Southern states, presaging the American Civil War. He envisioned that a touch "by the better angels of our nature" would "swell the chorus of the Union" to remind the nation's people of our common history, shared vision, and common destiny. Despite our perceived differences, Lincoln believed that whether through force or choice, each of our destinies is inextricably enmeshed with the fate of our nation. We are each a part of the soul of America. We share in its past, present, and future. Our better angels link us to the nation and its people. Our bonds may sometimes fracture, as happened only a month after Lincoln's inaugural speech when the Civil War began. But the vision of a united nation eventually won out. Deeper fractures exist today that touch every aspect of our lives, providing an opportunity, once again, to seek the aid of our better angels or spiritual Self whose unflappable vision of who we can be can help remake who we are.

Meeting the needs of a suffering nation and world requires those becoming aware of their "better angels" to circulate spiritually inspired thoughts and activities to serve the greater good for the greatest number. When using words such as "angels," "soul," and "spiritual," one is apt to assume a religious connotation, which is only one interpretation. These words — angel, soul, spirit — point to a vision of something more. Speaking of the angel or soul of an individual or nation identifies that aspect of each that is aware of its group identity and group relations. What we owe each other can only be answered by the person, organization, and nation becoming aware of themselves as human and divine: as a personality and soul. Calling upon the angels of our nature at a time of profound national strife, Lincoln reminded Americans of their spiritual destiny to become "...one Nation under God, indivisible, with liberty and justice for all." As souls, we remember unity even amidst differences. As souls, we respond vociferously with a willingness to shoulder responsibility and give our all when President John F. Kennedy asks in his 1961 inaugural address, "Ask not what your country can do for you — ask what you can do for your country." Invoking our better angels brings the common good into view with a clearsightedness that lights our path and reveals the steps we must take to heal people and the planet. It is not through the imposition of some particular method or formula to achieve this or that, although practical activities that solve world problems must necessarily develop. Instead, it is a focused and directed intention to grasp *the Good* to meet human and planetary needs that help humanity manifest its divinity, unity, and true identity as the one humanity. Then and only then can a new and better world appear.

UC Berkeley political scientists, analyzing datasets from the 1970s, lay bare a disturbing trend of declining confidence in institutions over the past five decades.[1] This study highlighted the erosion of public trust in various spheres of society, revealing a growing distrust for political (Presidency, Congress, Supreme Court, etc.) and nonpolitical (media, education, public schools, medicine, religion, law, etc.) institutions. Further, this distrust manifested along partisan lines, resulting in greater trust in "business, the police, religion, and the military" among Republicans compared to more confidence in "labor, the press, science, higher education, and public schools" among Democrats. The partisan divide, social mistrust, and overall decline in public trust in our nation's institutions impede effective governance, collaborative problem-solving, and the overall well-being of individuals, communities, and the nation.

When citizens witness leaders committing to the common good above personal gain, it becomes easier for individuals to practice civic virtue, contributing their best to the whole. We must be a nation of leaders working cooperatively to champion policies and practices prioritizing shared well-being and restoring the spiritual circulatory flow that streams through our planet with abundance sufficient to meet the needs of the many lives it nurtures — human and nonhuman. The ills of our society and diseases are directly attributable to the siphoning off and damming up of this universal abundance. We have unjustly enriched some at the expense of others based on national borders arrived at through violence and war, selfishness, and greed. Our rugged individualism, a term coined

---

1   Henry E. Brady, Thomas B. Kent; Fifty Years of Declining Confidence & Increasing Polarization in Trust in American Institutions. *Daedalus* 2022; 151 (4): 43–66. doi: https://doi.org/10.1162/daed_a_01943.

by President Herbert Hoover shortly before the start of the Great Depression, justifies and celebrates selfish misappropriation, misuse, and misdirection of resources to fulfill personal aims and ambitions. However, when constructively viewed in terms of time and place, Hoover's rugged individualism must be regarded as the right keynote sounded at the right time for what America faced, even if today we recognize the need for a more *cooperative* individualism capable of unleashing new potentialities just as surely as did Hoover's demand for self-reliance.

The individual's initiative and enterprise, seemingly divorced from the common good, built America. Today, group intent, focused, directed, and organized to achieve the common good can create a still better America. Shifting from a rugged to a *cooperative* individualism remedies the diseased and atrophied individualistic aspect of our consciousness, allowing something new and inspired to take its place. Real-world impact benefitting the many rather than the few can help restore trust in our institutions, heal the nation, and inspire others to practice civic virtue, contributing their best to the whole.

The rugged individualist in our nation's history has been rewarded for taking and not giving, accepting and not sharing, and grasping and not distributing. We must establish a new precedent for leadership. In *The Common Good*, Robert B. Reich calls for leadership to entail trusteeship. He says,

> *"Trusteeship should be baked into our understanding of successful leadership. Political victories that undermine trust in politics shouldn't be considered victories; they're net losses for society. Record corporate profits achieved by eroding the public's trust in business aren't successes; they're derelictions of duty. Lobbying and campaign donations that result in laws and regulations*

favoring the lobbyists and donors aren't triumphs if they weaken
public confidence in our democracy; they, too, are abject failures
of leadership."[2]

Trusteeship acknowledges a right of use and, at the same time, recognizes that we are not the bestower but the recipients of what has been given. As borrowers of spiritual gifts for earthly use, we learn to detach from an innate acquisitiveness, instead using what is needed to further our and others' spiritual betterment. The result is a lighter footprint in relationships with others and our environment, impulsed by mutuality rather than rugged individuality. Repurposing individualism for the common good means changing our leadership paradigm to reward selflessness and cooperation instead of personal and political gain.

As a result of our real and deeply felt pain, we sometimes use language that inadvertently distorts the work we must do. Using words like *toxic* to describe individuality and masculinity doesn't signal our collective need to provide a balance for expressed imbalances. Toxic individuality doesn't sound like it contains something worth salvaging. When something is deemed toxic or contaminated, we want to excavate and eradicate it if possible. Considering individuality or masculinity as poisonous can lead to an unfortunate situation of "throwing the baby out with the bath water." There are many societal imbalances between genders, classes, races, generations, political parties, college and non-college educated, religious values, urban and rural, labor and capital, and so on, requiring tempered resolution not to prolong people's misery but to ensure the preservation of the good and safe and sane destruction of the bad.

---

2   Reich, Robert B.. *The Common Good.* First edition. New York, Alfred A. Knopf, 2018.

Cooperative individualism acknowledges our need to break from the rugged individualism of the past and integrate these dualities within ourselves, institutions, and nations before a true world synthesis can be demonstrated fully. For this reason, prioritizing the common good, understood as a voluntary, self-initiated intent to develop one's capacities with an awareness of one's relationship to the whole, bridges present-day oppositions and helps realize an eventual and much hoped-for world unity. Evolving from a rugged to a *cooperative* individualism provides an opportunity to create a stable and adaptive transition to a new future, rebuilding institutions along more right lines and guided by a shared vision of *a more perfect Union.*

Individuality is a necessary stage that equips us to contribute the best of who we are to the whole. However, selfish individualism exacerbates our differences, leading to strife and division, whereas selfless individualism unites us for a shared purpose as a nation and world. Seeking *the Good*, we transform ourselves, becoming more fit to embody and demonstrate *the Good* for the common good. In doing so, we discover a unity of purpose to work alongside others to establish those conditions that confirm each person as an indissoluble part of the whole and provide them the social, economic, and political means to develop and contribute their best. Having discovered our better angels, we increasingly train our focus on *the Good,* conveyed to our minds through contact with this higher Self, to serve the common good, ending the personal desire life that creates, fortifies, and misappropriates *the Good* for selfish aims.

3.

"THE GOOD"

THE GOOD IS the unwavering, adaptive vision that has led humanity from one milestone to the next. It is the divine call to betterment to which the higher Self, innate within each of us, readily responds. Some call it freedom. It is the desire to free ourselves from the circumstances that limit us, to strive to realize our highest potential, to voyage into space, to build cities, to transport people over land and air to distances near or far, to develop technologies that make greater creativity more possible for more people. *The Good* evokes the inspirations that, when registered, adapted, and shared for the good of the human family and planetary life, deliver a life filled with beauty and peace for humankind.

Personalities, coordinated and effective, often self-serving but sometimes selfless, have shaped our world. Inspired by dimly grasped ideas, great men and women have set about conquering the world, freeing others dominated by the powerful, building empires, taking and not giving, and sometimes giving without asking for anything in return. The *something* innate within human beings — our better angels, souls, higher Self, spiritual, or divine natures — impulses our drive towards betterment, expressing desire, aspiration, and eventually the will-*to-Good*. Each progressive stage widens our vision and nurtures our capacity to serve others beyond ourselves — our family, community, nation, and world. The realizable *Good* is as much of the universal *Good* as humanity can grasp and make practicable at any time in human history. It is the Will of God materializing through humanity as goodwill exercised by the many and evoked by the will-*to-Good* of those identifying with the greater whole of which they are a part, the one humanity and one planet.

Up to this point, promoting the common good has been aspirational rather than practical, too often more optimistic than realistic, bandied about in times of national and world crises (wars, 9/11, the Great Depression, the coronavirus pandemic). Historically, groups have invoked conceptions of the common good to justify advances serving only their group, reinforcing existing inequities and discrimination against the most disadvantaged members of society. Too often, our nation has repeatedly asked the most needy among us to make sacrifices for the good of the whole, failing to recognize and respond to their swelling unmet needs. As a result, *the Good,* intended to serve the benefit of all, is instead selfishly interpreted for some part rather than the whole, intensifying division and separation.

Perhaps more than any other nation in the history of the world, America epitomizes the heights of a well-organized, abundantly aspirational society. After all, the American Dream's promise of a better life for all remains a clarion call throughout the world despite its seeming unattainability for the most vulnerable among us. Writing in his 1931 best-selling book, *Epic of America*, Historian

James Truslow Adams coined the phrase the "American Dream," describing it as

"not a dream of motor cars and high wages merely, but a dream of social order in which each man and each woman shall be able to attain to the fullest stature of which they are innately capable, and be recognized by others for what they are, regardless of the fortuitous circumstances of birth or position."[3]

Thus, relying upon only an aspirational vision of the common good would resemble faith without works, lacking the pragmatic will-*to-Good* required to ensure the promise that its originator intended: creating a social, economic, and political order that allows each person to reach their highest potential and, thereby, give their best to the nation.

The will to inaugurate *the Good* for the Commons generates the purposeful solutions to our most significant challenges, collectively orchestrated across all sectors of human living — social, economic, cultural, and political. Motivated by an aspirational view of the common good, we've advocated for a sense of "community" or "belonging" without providing the ideas, leadership, and financial resources needed to manifest *the Good* for the Commons in practical ways. The idea, of course, and the activities it spurred weren't for naught. Such a radical idea must begin with widespread enthusiasm to seal permanently in the public consciousness even while its implementation remains unrealized.

Too often, what is good for the Commons is gleaned separately from quotas, most active voting blocs, or highly resourced special

---

3   Adams, James Truslow. The Epic of America. Boston: Little, Brown, and Company, 1931.

interest groups. *The Good* hovers above humanity, inspiring, guiding, and evolving it from one stage to the next. *The Good* envelops the emerging ideas that, when rightly grasped and effectively implemented for the common good, make possible humanity's continued development and eventual realization and commitment to give the best of themselves to the whole. The common good is, therefore, not the sum of individual interests but the guidepost for determining the needs of individuals, groups, and nations. Contact with our group-oriented higher Self reveals to us *the Good*, provided we do not pervert the ideas intended to serve the whole to fulfill personal preferences, either low or high.

We can begin with the premise of sharing the world's abundance according to need and ensure that what we provide permits members of the Commons to continue to develop themselves and, in doing so, realize what they can give back to the whole of which they increasingly know themselves to be a part. Until and unless the sectors influencing our lives — economic, social, religious, political, scientific, educational, etc. — are directed by leaders motivated by *the Good* and striving to adapt it to present needs in practical ways, our society will continue to create winners and losers. Yet creating and maintaining the common good also requires the cooperative efforts of some, often of many, people. When leaders fail in their duties, promoting self-interests over the public good, it tears at the social fabric, crystallizes competition, and erodes civic responsibility. Reviving the common good requires a definite reorientation for Americans enthralled by rugged individualism and its illusory spoils of wealth and power that prioritize individual rights as if such can exist independently of an orderly, safe, and stable nation. To effectuate the peace and tranquility all human beings everywhere crave, a *cooperative* individualism oriented to the common good is a definite step forward towards making concrete progress in realizing *the Good*.

According to a survey conducted in October 2020, which asked respondents to what extent they agreed with the statement, "I'm very troubled by the moral state of our country," seventy-one percent (71%) agreed or completely agreed, and only 13% disagreed.[4]

A plea for moral leadership indicates a reorientation of the priorities that result in divisive politics, striking inequality, and social and environmental degradation, demanding more unifying and productive ideas and activities that benefit the many rather than the few. Bishop William J. Barber II, Director and founder of Yale Divinity School's Center for Public Theology & Public Policy and self-described moral movement leader, posits that moral questions, derived either by faith, commitment to the constitution, or a belief in the "moral arc of the universe, must intersect with public policy." He says, "We don't ask "Is it right or is it left? Is it Democrat or is it Republican?"... You ask, "Does it establish justice? ... Does this promote general welfare? Does it ensure equal protection under the law, regardless of creed, regardless of sexuality?"[5]

Questions of morality presuppose some understanding of *the Good*, indicating receptivity to a pattern of spiritually orienting, universal ideas that sustain humanity's urge to cultivate and express its higher capacities. Sharing his ideas on service in "An Ideal of Service to Our Fellow Man," Albert Einstein says, "What is moral is not the divine, but rather a purely human matter, albeit

---

4 Making Caring Common. (2021, December). Do Americans really care for each other? What Unites Us—And Divides Us. https://mcc.gse.harvard.edu/reports/do-americans-care-about-each-other.

5 Gallup, Jasmine. "Rev. William Barber Reflects on 10th Anniversary of Moral Movement." *Indy Week*, 26 Apr. 2023. https://indyweek.com/news/northcarolina/moral-mondays-anniversary-barber-reflects/. Accessed 23 September 2023.

the most important of all human matters." [6]

Morality, in essence, is our individual and collective interpretation and adaptation of the will of God or what Einstein calls "the most profound reason" manifesting as creation. Human morality depends on an intelligent receptivity and distribution of inspired or divine ideas in cooperation with the Reason, Intelligence, or God that manifests Itself in nature. Morality indicates a conscious recognition that there is a pattern upon which creation exists and our ability to become aware of and a conscious participant to further Its ends. A moral person understands this divine Plan as it conditions life upon our planet and bends all toward justice. To the degree that each of us submits to this conditioning, we can more fully participate in the purposes for which this creative intelligence aims.

The outstanding achievements in science, technology, and medicine that demonstrate a greater awareness of world issues, longer life expectancies, and modes of transportation linking each to every part of the planet are part of the hovering spiritual gifts contacted by focused and dedicated minds for the use and betterment of humanity. It is, however, apparent that such discoveries have been usurped for selfish purposes, providing power and wealth to the few rather than flourishing to the many. Reinstating the common good as part of our lexicon alongside a willed intent to manifest *the Good* and identifying leaders in every field of human endeavor who align with it is the first step in reclaiming *the Good* for all, each of us becoming a steward of our planet's resources providing for our collective well-being. Distribution according to need, reestablishing the circulatory flow that brings betterment to

---

6   Einstein, Albert. "An Ideal of Service to Our Fellow Man." *NPR*, NPR, 28 May 2005, www.npr.org/2005/05/28/4670423/an-ideal-of-service-to-our-fellow-man.

all planetary life, including the one humanity manifests *the Good* continuously improving life upon our planet until such time that what is visible more accurately reflects the sublime.

4.

OBSTACLES TO "THE GOOD"

THE AMERICAN IMAGINATION

Creative imagination is a perceptive faculty that negotiates between our group conscious higher Self and self-conscious personality. Within the American imagination exists the collective creativity, innovation, and visionary thinking that has characterized the United States since its inception. It encompasses the ability of Americans to envision and pursue new ideas, technologies, and social structures, often leading to both significant advancements and, at times, negative consequences. It is the source of the myriad and competing imaginings whose source is *the Good* but which are manipulated and colored by the purity (or lack thereof) of each person's heart and mind. Responsible equally for technological advancements and space exploration as displacement of indigenous (native) Americans and nuclear weapons, the American imagination contains the good and bad of our storied past and possibilities of our yet-to-be-realized future. To manifest *the Good* necessitates correct response to new ideas, requiring diligence to recognize and interpret new possibilities that would improve life for all, overcoming the self-centeredness that clouds perceptions, keeping some too small and making others too great. In one instance, people fail to recognize the contribution they can and must make. In the latter case, people become self-important, attempting to do more than what is needed and what is theirs to do.

Many obstacles to the correct perception and interpretation exist that prevent the entrance of *the Good*. These are, as the Buddha taught so long ago, the diversity of forms with which we identify, including ours and others' personalities, identities, organizations, ideologies, nations, etc., that often distort *the Good* intended for all to something lesser to serve an individual, group, or nation's desires and aspirations. Understanding these challenges can better equip us to manifest *the Good* for the common good.

Three categories of obstacles make accessing and manifesting *the Good* more difficult, including faulty equipment, faulty interpretation, and promiscuity. Understanding the obstacles each of these categories represents helps us identify our individual and collective need to think, reorient our focus to include the common good of which the individual is an indispensable part, and learn to act intelligently rather than indiscriminately to materialize *the Good*.

FAULTY EQUIPMENT

We still need to develop our mind's capacity for group awareness, which is the ability to think from the universal to the particular instead of the part to the whole. Our current default is to think first and foremost about the individual and gradually extend beyond personal concerns to include others — family, community, nation, and world. Since *the Good* concerns only the whole, it either fails to penetrate stridently individualistic minds or such people incorrectly interpret it for selfish benefit. We react emotionally or unintelligently to *the Good* until we build the capacity to *think*, which means accurately interpreting those aspects of *the Good* the higher Self reveals, helping us discern the Real from the Unreal. *The Good* provides ideas and incentives for service to humankind, and being either unaware, unresponsive, or uninterested in the good of others, the selfish personality or self-conscious mind becomes a shield, preventing us from sensing *the Good* accurately and intelligently to make use of it for shared purpose and common good. As Ito-Morales indicated in a 2022 study of Japan's handling of Covid-19, its concept of self-restraint distinguished its approach, adding to the debate between the more communitarian common good approach in the East and the West's emphasis on individual rights and freedom.[7]

Introducing the Japanese term *jishuku*, meaning self (ji自) abstention (shuku 粛), which embodies the idea of voluntary self-restraint, Morales provides a way to balance our rugged individualism with a willingness to share in the suffering of others. Voluntary abstention comes into play when our more typical individual self-assertion might cause others harm. Recognizing that insisting on our rights and freedom can harm or exacerbate existing harm and choosing to abstain is *jishuku*. It develops from the coexisting realities of realizing one's individuality and commonality, which education

---

7   Ito-Morales, K. "Individual Rights Vs. Common Good? A Case Study on Japanese Self-Restraint (jishuku) and COVID-19". Asian Studies, vol. 10, no. 1, Jan. 2022

can facilitate by helping each person reach their highest potential, knowing themselves to be an integral part of a greater whole. When Walt Whitman attests, "(I am large, I contain multitudes.)" ("Song of Myself, 51"), its implication is not that he is a mix of many varied identities (race, gender, class, etc.) but that he contains the various individualized expressions of the entire creation within himself. He is himself and *all*. It is a duality — the self and the whole — that permits a more fully realized individual expression because knowing ourselves as *this and that* — the part and the whole — multiplies and improves our individual and collective capacities and impacts through each group member's similarly oriented thought and activity as they seek to implement *the Good*. Becoming conscious of the common good makes it possible for us to be as secure in our individuality as we are in our commonality. We are ourselves, and that self contains *multitudes*. We become genuinely harmless because our consciousness includes others, and we recognize that the individual can't thrive without a healthy body — a family, community, state, nation, and world. Our ability to stabilize our thoughts according to the needs of the whole conditions us to become less self-referential, determined to have our way, and therefore capable of imbuing our lives and activities with self-forgetfulness, harmlessness, and right speech.

FAULTY INTERPRETATION

As our minds become more receptive to ideas achieved when emotional reactivity lessens and quiet moments still the mind, faulty equipment becomes less of an impediment. Instead, we now face the more arduous task of addressing our duplicity. Remembering that *the Good* embodies those emerging ideas available to us for use by us — individually and collectively — to serve the common good, we begin to recognize the extent to which our self-centered illusions and delusions have clouded our perception, leading us to misinterpret, misapply, and misdirect our thoughts. Collective imaginings, containing every desire and aspiration, whether high or low, deflect and crowd out *the Good*. Only a developed and sustained contact with our higher Self restores its viability, making it possible to know what is the common good. Although rugged individualists may grasp *the Good*, they cannot accurately interpret it because they don't yet think about the common good but only of themselves and those they love. On the other hand, the cooperative and group-conscious individual becomes a conduit for *the Good* because they begin to think less of themselves and, therefore, are less prone to selfish distortion. By correctly recognizing, interpreting, and striving to implement an aspect of *the Good*, *cooperative* personalities destroy some small part of the collective desires and aspirations presently preventing widespread implementation of the common good for all.

Desires

The American imagination is the most materialistic of any nation. It contains the stuff of every dream, desire, and wish of every citizen. It is a petri dish of successes, failures, unrequited pining, heartbreak, bad decisions, regrettable choices, unfulfilled hopes, and our lowest and highest aspirations. Each longing contributes to a vast miasma that drives us in many directions without moving us forward. Like *the Good*, these fictions also collect and hover above us but instead block out much of the light, transporting *the Good*. When some of *the Good* pierces through, and we use it correctly for human betterment, the air above us becomes clearer and more refined. Thus, the clearing away through correct apprehension and adaptation of *the Good* for human and planetary betterment allows for more of *the*

Good to flow to and through humanity. When, instead, we corrupt *the Good*, splitting it off according to each person's selfish interpretation and self-serving need, the desires created often fail (thankfully!) to achieve their goal and instead accumulate in the collective imagination, making it more difficult for us to contact *the Good*.

Part of our task in achieving the common good, requiring ongoing recognition, adaptation, and demonstration of *the Good*, is to voluntarily and willingly sacrifice our varied desires and aspirations to clear the air above so that all can see *the Good* more clearly and work unitedly to make it our shared reality. Contact with *the Good* through our higher Selves initiates a practice of self-discipline that, in due time, controls cravings, tempers emotions, and decentralizes self-referencing thoughts. When impulsed by the higher Self or soul, conformity to the common good becomes possible due to increased exposure to *the Good*, participation in its manifestation, and subsequent devotion to it due to taking part in initiating its positive effects.

Aspirations

The ideal is the sphere of the soul. Whitman's "multitudes" describe a man trying to understand himself as part of a greater whole that is not only evident in the diversity of people, animals, plants, and the universe outside of him but an identity taking shape within as well. Each of us is individualized in our consciousness and equally capable of becoming conscious of the multitudes. Unity in multiplicity. Outwardly different, inwardly one. Our ability to recognize the essential duality between the individual and the common good (the part and the whole) and a willingness to sacrifice personal gain for the greater good transforms desire into aspiration. Between complete selfishness and selflessness, aspiration heralds the ability to bridge the gap between soul and personality, indicating the capacity to envision *the Good* and a willingness to eventually become its creative agent.

To aspire is to revel in potentialities, imagining the good, the true, and the beautiful. Aspiration alone, however, cannot materialize the vision. The will-*to-Good* must accompany aspiration, providing the requisite incentive to build, rebuild, and build again. Unlike personal will, the will-*to-Good* denotes the intent to bring about a shared purpose instead of what one desires or aspires to achieve only for oneself. The truth is that committing ourselves to a shared purpose helps us realize our greatest potential. We often find that when others' well-being is at stake, we can give more than we thought we had to offer. We find strength in helping others find fulfillment, discovering that we are somehow becoming capable of assisting others to meet their needs. Our striving for the common good brings out our best. Recognizing and responding to human needs helps us let go, step-by-step, of personal desire, personal aspiration, and YES! personal will. Seeking to meet the needs of the common good absorbs each of our "little wills" into a potent will of the people, magnifying each exponentially to create solutions where there had been stagnation and opportunity where there had been hopelessness.

Today, we are witnessing the limits of aspiration without the coordinated will to enact *the Good*. Christians proclaim, "Faith without works is dead." *The Good* encroaches upon us from every direction, igniting our spirits, cultivating our minds, and relentlessly urging conformity to its realizable perfection. Without *the Good*, the spirit of humanity would atrophy and die of its own volition. *The Good* is our hope for tomorrow, a glimpse of what is to come but not a guarantee. We who can see must learn to act while, at the same time, dissipating the miasmas of our collective imaginings antagonistic to the common good. Undeveloped and individualistic thoughts distort *the Good*, keeping a more perfect world at bay. Still, *the Good* remains the *Idea* that Gamaliel Bradford, Jr., biographer and critic, attests in "The American Idealist,"

> "*...can never die, never lose its influence over mankind, never cease to be the mainspring of all that is accomplished in the world, — of all progress, of all virtue, of all happiness. It clothes itself in many forms. It puts on and casts off religions and philosophies like worn and faded garments. All these change, but the Idea remains the same. Something outside, something beyond, something larger than itself, humanity must have to strive for, to hope for.* [8]

We can only clear the detritus of misapplied and misused remnants of ideas born from the *Idea* and intended for all when we relinquish the desire life that perverts them for selfish aims. Our unwillingness to share, distribute, and cooperate is a definite obstacle that we compensate for with pain and suffering evidenced by our present conditions, including rising economic and social inequality, climate catastrophe, forced immigrant displacement due to discrimination, poverty, and violence, political polarization, and nationalism driven by fear and hate. The darker side of American aspiration denies the perniciousness of racism, anti-immigrant sentiments, nationalism masked as patriotism, and hatred or intolerance based on a belief that the American ideal defines an ideal American identified more by fortuities of birth rather than values of choice. Affirming the common good in thought and action permits decision-makers and

---

8   Bradford, Gamaliel, Jr. "The American Idealist." *The Atlantic*, July 1892, https://www.theatlantic.com/magazine/archive/1892/07/the-american-idealist/634692/. Accessed 25 December 2023.

the people of goodwill, receptive to *the Good*, dedicated to humanity, and capable of intelligently grasping what is and what can be to rebuild the culture of our nation by promoting the conditions that yield our best and restrain our worst.

Having and Not-Having

Having and not-having equally provide opportunities to develop qualities that draw out our best. Materially controlled, however, we often equate not-having with pain and suffering, refusing to recognize its beneficence. We lament the grist of life even as it purifies desires and helps unleash hidden capacities that would otherwise remain undeveloped unless and until our backs are against the wall. Through pain and suffering, we let go of the nonessentials. We lose ourselves to discover the common good and the one essential and universal Self. Dedicated to the common good, we awaken to others' suffering, to which we must learn to respond wisely. Appropriate intervention can only be ascertained when *harmlessness* conditions our thoughts and behaviors. A non-critical spirit, affirming each person's divine essence coupled with a loving understanding of their developmental stage, can reveal whether they presently suffer needlessly or as a means to secure greater freedom for themselves.

Each of us confronts life's successes and failures to develop our individual personality and awaken us to the reality of our divine nature: the soul. Traversing the vicissitudes of life cannot be avoided if we are to become and express outwardly the truth that we contact inwardly. Presently, group impulse and incentive, particularly among selfishly oriented coordinated personalities, remains a formidable hindrance to restoring the divine circulatory flow that unites, uplifts, and incentivizes everyone to contribute the best within them to the whole. Service to humanity necessarily indicates the need to construct all relationships to awaken each — individuals, groups, and nations — to their divinity and responsibility for right expression as parts of a greater whole. Through harmlessness, we learn to take the right action at the right time and for the right reason. Further, we recognize pain and suffering as redemptive when justly endured and regressive when unjustly imposed or permitted.

"Mothers love their sons but raise their daughters" is a phrase heard often within the black community, giving voice to many black women's deeply felt experience post-Civil Rights as they began to advance in education and workplaces. The more ground they gained, the less likely they were to find black men with whom they felt "equally yoked" in drive, ambition, ability, stability, maturity, and willingness to shoulder responsibility. These were not necessarily born of personal failings, as most women understood, but unrealized possibilities due, at least in part, to oppression and subjugation. A 2010 *Journal of Family Psychology* study assessed 1,500 adolescents to determine the extent to which "African American mothers differentially socialize their girls and boys."[9]

The researchers concluded "that later-born boys had fewer chores, argued more with their mothers, lived in less cognitively stimulating homes, and were not allowed to make the same decisions as were the girls or firstborn boys at the same age." Their lower achievement and higher externalizing behaviors or "acting out," the study attributed directly to parenting differences. Having observed the damaging results of "loving" mothers and paternal systems, I can attest to our collective need to adjust these practices. I've known young men (and dated one) whose mothers refused to let them fail, experience discomfort if they could prevent it, entangled

9   Mandara, Jelani, et al. "Do African American Mothers Really 'Love' Their Sons and 'Raise' Their Daughters?" *Journal of Family Psychology*, vol. 24, no. 1, Feb. 2010, pp. 41–50, https://doi.org/10.1037/a0018072.]

themselves in the emotional ups and downs of their sons, and ultimately did for them the things that they could and should do for themselves, whatever the consequences. When a former boyfriend's mom told me how she would leave work and drive thirty minutes to her son's high school on the other side of town to take him the lunch he forgot, not once or twice but often, I was confused. In high school, I made my breakfast, packed my lunch, and, on occasion, when I forgot it, negotiated with the cafeteria to repay at a later date or borrowed money from a friend at school. We discussed why she felt the need to usurp his right to suffer, grow, and figure things out. I remember when it dawned on me how his mom's love towards him had not only inadvertently confirmed her lack of faith in his abilities to *do* life but more egregiously robbed him of faith in himself. He resented her for making him feel helpless and despised himself for continuing to need her long past the natural stage of maturation. She loved him deeply. Yet he *felt* unloved, creating a vicious cycle.

Institutional paternalism operates in a very similar way. America's paternalistic economic, social, and political systems are ripe for restructuring. We must balance the goals of supporting people at all levels, creating harmless systems structured in ways that recognize where people are while providing the practical help they need to ease them stage by stage along the continuum to a life of dignity and purpose. Given too much, we dull self-will. Given too little, we inculcate and inflame antisocial personalities or permit needless suffering. Either approach impedes proper human maturation.

Working at a residential high school during a period of immense change (for the better), staff had to confront the ingrained paternalism of an institution created over seventy years ago to serve at-risk boys. Since many of our students had a history of trauma, convincing staff that what they most needed was so-called tough love was challenging. People of goodwill, which everyone who worked there most certainly was, are desperate to end human suffering. Tough love combines love, which recognizes pain, with the wisdom that identifies the suffering and its cause. Tough love, or better still, *wise* love is harmless. It steadies our hand and ensures an appropriate response according to the need. It is *tough*, arresting behaviors, habits, and mindsets antagonistic to the common good and *love* because it is ultimately restorative and instructive, encouraging the child's or adult's further development along more right lines beneficial both to them and others. It is adaptive. The more we collectively stopped *loving* and instead "raising" (which is really true love!) our charges, the more their behaviors, attitudes, and belief in themselves began to change for the better. Our job was not to alleviate life's challenges but to provide them with the resources and self-knowledge to help them face every obstacle and trust themselves enough to rise to the occasion. Even the young men who seemed lazy, disengaged, and unmotivated began to find their footing. It wasn't simply a matter of being challenged. It was a matter of being *seen*. And not just seen in terms of their present flaws but the person they were desperate to become.

When attempting to control others' behaviors or life outcomes, we inevitably stop them — at least temporarily — from having the experiences and learning the lessons life intends to teach them. At one end of the spectrum, there are wilderness therapy programs that kidnap teenagers exhibiting at-risk behaviors at the behest of concerned parents and state-sanctioned compelled treatment for people with untreated mental illness or unhealthy drugs and alcohol use. On the other end are the many insidious ways that caring adults attempt to manipulate and control children to obtain desired outcomes. We may argue that these results — more well-behaved humans, better students, a more satisfying life — are in the child's or adult's best interest, and indeed they are, but if and when achieved, they often prove unsustainable. Purely focusing on getting others to do what we want them to do or becoming who we want them to be denies the soul within them. Instead of helping them recognize this inner master, we become its typically unwise substitute. If and when we withdraw from this person, or they leave our care, their lives naturally revert to what they were before our interference, or they fall apart without our guidance. We observed this for many of our students within six months of graduation, forcing us to re-evaluate how we interacted with and influenced them while enrolled in our program. The proper role for others who genuinely need our help is to recognize that our primary goal in their lives is to put them in touch with the master within. Then they develop in their own time into self-aware, self-directed, self-expressing, and contributing members of our world.

It has become commonplace today for people to talk about their "privilege," which includes an array of characteristics related to race ("white privilege"), sex ("male privilege"), gender ("cisgender privilege"), ability ("able-bodied privilege") that predominate at this time in human history. Well-meaning people remind us to "check your privilege" as a conduit to empathy and compassion. Our efforts to raise awareness of the needs of the most vulnerable who lack the good fortune to be born into a loving family or familial wealth or fail to embody their historical period's most preeminent characteristics ignore that having and not having both carry distinct challenges and opportunities to further our development. Not having can release us from attachment, bringing to life a greater sense of who we are when we lack possessions, don't fit in with those around us, and must learn to stand alone.

On the other hand, having it all also carries moral quandaries and hazards that must be faced. Both having and not having are equally constructive when viewed as opportunities to find release from one stage of human experience into another, leading to identification with the common good. Labels of "privilege" glorify having to the extent that we associate the absence of all that we desire or aspire to with pain and suffering. When we become more adept at contacting and correctly implementing *the Good*, we learn the wisdom of detachment, dispassion, and discrimination, as the Buddha taught, which inhibits a rush to judgment and impulsivity in action, develops reticence in speech, and refrains from criticism, resulting in loving and wise action.

Siddhartha Gautama, the Buddha, Whose teachings preceded the influx of His Brother, the Christ's message of Love, taught us the path to wisdom. He was born into a wealthy family, surrounded by opulence. Perhaps recognizing his potential for empathy from birth, His father sought to protect Him from witnessing the world's sufferings, fearful that if He saw them, He might give up his royal duties to understand and help end pain and suffering. Having disavowed a life of luxury, the Buddha became enlightened, revealing to Him that it was humanity's attachment to our material (personality) self and its fluctuating desires, attracting and repelling, rather than our spiritual selves (higher Self or spirit) that is the source of our pain and suffering. The Buddha offered an end to pain and suffering, not by giving people all they desired but by revealing that personal desire could be extinguished by identification with and becoming a proper channel for *the Good*.

We readily admit that not having can thwart realized ambition, but the ways that having can sometimes diminish empathy, destroy relationships, and manufacture a false sense of identity often escape us. How difficult a choice is it for us lesser buddhas to sacrifice the comfort of having — education, good food, love and companionship, security, influence, intellectual stimulation, and existential safety to share in "[t]he fellowship of Christ's sufferings?" Not-having and having can present equally challenging obstacles to recognizing ourselves as part of a greater whole and prioritizing the common good over personal gain. Not-having, when unjustly perpetuated, can reinforce self-preservation, negating the common good, as Abraham Maslow surmised, in part, in his hierarchy of needs, distinguishing between deficiency needs and growth needs. Although Maslow's theory presented the stages — physiological, safety, belonging and love, social needs or esteem, self-actualization, and transcendence — as ascending developmental stages that human beings pass having satisfied the lower level needs before attaining the next level, this isn't necessarily the case. There are many instances in which the poor, marginalized, and disfavored demonstrate a relentless capacity to merge completely — body, mind, and soul — with the needs of others, reminding us of the need to distinguish between appearances and reality, between the lower self and higher Self, personality and soul.

A wise person recognizes that obstacles don't need to be removed unless they are arbitrary and discriminatory. They see life as the crucible in which human beings make themselves and discover capacities they can only develop through living, relating, and aspiring to be, do, and have something more. Desire, aspiration, and the will-*to-Good* are facets of our innate spirituality, guiding us by degrees from focusing on ourselves, then extending concern to those we love, and eventually to identification with the many lives on our planet. To adequately recognize the depth of an individual's spiritual wealth, indicating their capacity to serve the common good, we must look beyond the presence or absence of material possessions or extrinsic esteem.

Too often, conversations about privilege and the social and economic advantages it provides mask the natural tendency shared by all human beings to choose ourselves over others, use our skills, whether god-given or pruned through grit and perseverance for personal gain, and shirk our responsibility to sacrifice our comforts (however minimal they seem) to lead, leaving the ruthlessly ambitious and ruggedly individualistic to delude and distort the will of the people. Every person who has envisioned a brighter tomorrow and senses somewhat *the Good* awaiting humanity's response has a duty and responsibility to join with like-minded others to bring about the common good because we *see* human suffering in its many forms, and we know *the Good* that is possible. Focused on the collective good will reveal new possibilities to humanity in which neither having nor not-having will prove adequate to distract or dissuade us from working together to achieve the greatest good for the greatest number.

PROMISCUITY

Within American society, freedom is generally confused with license. Too often, a demand for freedom masks a desire to abdicate one's responsibility to others. License prioritizes our individual needs and wants irrespective of how others are affected. Some gun owners — thankfully, not all — insist on the license to carry or concealed carry without the needling interference of background checks, waiting periods, or grappling with the increased proliferation of guns, including assault weapons that make mass murder easier to carry out. Sexual license and abortion insist on bodily autonomy, unwilling primarily to wrestle intelligently to establish those customs that help make us what we can be and not merely confirm what we are.

When attitudes to daily living change, indicating spiritual values that recognize and assert the group good and are reinforced through education, our understanding of sex, marriage, parenthood, family life, work, and citizenship will radically transform. Our failure to recognize that we are each a part of a greater whole — a family, community, nation, and world — makes us mistake freedom as license. The dichotomy between freedom and license appears everywhere. Many people subvert responsibility due to ignorance of their relation to the whole: the one humanity and one planet. With them, the wise must be compassionate, patient, and just, understanding that upon the evolutionary path, all people appear at various grades and levels, indicating conscious conformity and expression of *the Good*, but are nonetheless expanding their consciousness to enable them to willingly take on ever greater responsibility for the destiny of humankind.

For the more aspirational and, therefore, emotional, license avoids the imposition of the lower mind's discriminating thought, which naturally dampens the high-highs of the feeling nature and equally tempers the low-lows. In other cases, among the more mental types, license permits them to neglect their duties, sometimes refusing to take part in the more mundane aspects of living, including marriage and parenthood, preferring unrelenting pursuits of world adventure and excitement instead. People, divorced from knowledge and commitment to the Commons, take license, consciously or unconsciously subverting group needs to fulfill personal desires. Through increasingly intelligent choice and wise discernment, we recognize that we are never free so long as we don't control but are controlled by what we desire to have or rid ourselves of. Undertaking responsibility soon becomes automatic because we have disciplined ourselves through practicing self-forgetfulness, harmlessness, and right speech. We learn to serve authentically by sacrificing getting our way and prioritizing instead the common good.

The American imagination, containing our collective desires and aspirations, high and low, houses many promiscuities.

Promiscuous derives its meaning from the Latin *promiscuus*, meaning "without distinction, taken from every different type." Other meanings include "indiscriminate," "not selective," and "consisting of parts, elements, or individuals of different kinds brought together **without order** [emphasis mine]." Amidst the current societal chaos facing the United States in which the old order upon which we have long relied is in demise, we can see the faint outlines of a new nation built on right relationships between people and right thoughts and actions that promote the common good. People of goodwill and loving understanding work tirelessly in every field of human endeavor to bring order out of chaos. These servers of humanity always stand for *the Good*, educating, inspiring, and helping to mitigate the harm caused by nihilists whose preference is to lay waste to everything without assessing what, if anything, is worth salvaging and others determinedly clinging to past relics, insisting that the way forward is, in reality, a return to some past for which many attest we've outgrown. Hence, a reordering of American society to benefit the common good requires us to learn and adapt a discriminating process that advances a shared goal, allowing us to rebuild, preserving what is good, beautiful, and true as a foundation upon which to build the new that more closely approximates *the Good*.

Concerning Relationships

Indiscriminate relationships and activities undermine the common good. Too often we base our relationships on associations that amplify personalities instead of the good of the whole. Many of us, increasingly aware of and responsive to the needs of the common good, fall somewhere in the middle. Sometimes, we find ourselves overcommitted to people, ideologies, systems, and associations of every kind that reinforce our selfish interests (belonging, like-mindedness, familiarity, exclusivity, etc.), leaving little room to discover our path of least resistance to service. Shifting from promiscuous to purposeful relationships puts us in contact with the people and groups needing our contribution and those we need to further develop our capacity to serve. This new basis for relationships centered on the good of the whole helps groups and their members better serve the common good attracted as they are by a shared goal that concentrates and directs their individual and group purpose, strengthening and multiplying its achievement. Like an interest-bearing account, the results of the many individuals impelled by *the Good* are cumulative, allowing many groups working toward a shared purpose to achieve what would otherwise be impossible for any one group or solitary individuals to do.

Sometimes, where we are differs from where we think we should be. We imagine and therefore limit our possibilities when deciding that we are more fit to serve — more often than not — at only the highest rungs of society, accumulating a vast wealth that, quite naturally, we'd pledge to give away in fellowship with the most brilliant people because — of course — they are us! Few of us imagine toiling nameless and unknown in the dimmest corners of society. If we find ourselves in these places, we will likely spend much energy planning and trying to escape our circumstances and fit ourselves to serve where our service isn't needed. Alternatively, some continue to serve in ways better left to others, spread themselves thin attempting to be everyone's everything, and thereby waste time and energy, diminishing *the Good* that might otherwise flow through them and their group.

When teaching at the all-boys residential high school in Northern California, students, discovering I was an attorney, would first marvel at the idea, asking if I would represent them if such an unfortunate occasion arose. After a while, their questions became accusatory, *"Why are you teaching?"* as if to suggest that I had done something really, *really* bad that prevented me from practicing law or that I had simply lost my mind. Students desperately wanting to "make it," to "get my fam up out da hood," and to prove to themselves and others that they had what it takes and weren't as disposable as the world sometimes made them feel thought I had to be crazy to walk away from the prestige and the money they were sure all lawyers made. *"Why would you leave all that to teach?"* was the question they wanted (and sometimes demanded) me to answer.

Being a lawyer was always about something other than the money for me. I went into law to be a public defender. When I became a criminal defense attorney in Detroit in the late '90s, a first-year teacher's salary was probably more than what I made. I never aspired to BigLaw and have the student debt to prove it. Attending a top-20 law school, however, as I did, funnels graduates into BigLaw, Wall Street, elected office (a classmate spent our final year running for and eventually winning a congressional seat), and judicial clerkships, so-called elite positions. Such influential positions are the image my students had in mind when trying to determine what I had left behind to work for lesser pay, lower status, and potentially a lot more stress. I tried to explain to them that I found myself teaching because I had responded to a need, nothing more, nothing less. Unsurprisingly, this failed to satisfy many of them.

Before joining the staff at this school, I was asked to mentor a student, to which I reluctantly agreed. Hanging out on campus with him for nearly a year helped me identify a need to which I found myself capable and willing to respond. I was learning how to serve, spontaneously and willingly, even at the cost of my comfort (after teaching in the '90s, I had sworn that I would never again enter the classroom), my often grandiose visions of serving in ways that necessarily included a quiet assurance of having made a difference in world affairs, and in a place more conducive to the life I was used to living. These imaginings can and do prevent even the most committed servers from contributing their best, unaware that not only is service what we give to others but what we get in return. Responding to the call to serve absorbs us more fully into communion with the Commons, accelerating our capacity to intuit *the Good* and rightly interpret it. In this way, serving wherever we find ourselves based on a growing awareness of right relationships as opposed to our more typical indiscriminate ones works to expand the range of our contacts and increase our capacity to serve.

Promiscuous relationships are the opposite of sacred or right relationships. Indiscriminate relationships lack order because we seek them out according to our desires and aspirations rather than for the common good. They are fluid, changing, groping, and impermanent. In other words, indiscriminate relationships are not built to last. They are founded upon personal, social, and cultural identities and not our common good, which is the goal of right relationships. Relying predominantly upon incidental (race, sex, nationality, class) or culturally expedient identities (gender, politics, religion) to unite a nation cannot succeed. Their changeability prohibits reliance upon them to forge an American identity. We can be "all the things," a multiplicity of races, sexes, genders, religions, political parties, ethnicities, classes, interests, and abilities while, at the same time, striving to become one consciousness united for the common good. Thus, those discovering *the Good* know that personal sacrifice for the Commons is needed. Sacer, the Latin word meaning "to make whole," is the root word for sacrifice. Through sacrifice — voluntarily made due to some understanding of *the Good* and a growing love for the one humanity — we begin to repurpose ambitions and aspirations to achieve outcomes inclusive of the needs of the Commons rather than advancing a more narrow achievement for some people and some groups.

New affinities based on right relations provide an improved way to organize individuals from all walks of life, groups, and institutions according to a shared ideal. Such groupings will share a unity of purpose but not necessarily uniformity in methods to achieve it. It focuses our attention on essentials instead of nonessentials, making it possible to work "across the aisle." In our conversations and interactions with others, we don't allow theirs or our own identities and associations to define who we are. Instead, we look deeper, asking questions and interrogating our own agendas to unearth each other's growing awareness of what is essential to human flourishing. There are people within all political parties, enterprises, churches, governments, and nations receptive to *the Good* and bending every effort to create a better world for all. Discovering those alongside whom we can work is fundamental to reorienting our ambitions and aspirations. Such new associations exponentially expand the depth and breadth of service for each and for this formidable group of world servers as a whole.

Adhering to indiscriminate relationships means that those emerging ideas that must be perceived, interpreted, and intelligently put to use by human beings often die on the vine. These attractive and magnetic ideas too often need more traction and ultimately fade into the recesses of experience, awaiting another opportunity for development. We all have had ideas that we thought could relieve one or another issue. Bolstered by courage, we may have dared to share them only to be met with blank stares or the enthusiasm common among armchair quarterbacks, willing to critique but not necessarily suit up. And among people taking the field and ready for battle, they insist upon *their* battle, *their* way. We negate what we could accomplish because of our refusal or inability to discern what is essential, missing the opportunity to align with others who — if we could but see it — share our dream.

Concerning Activity (Busyness)

Standing in the way of the common good are superfluous attachments related to temporal identities and the flurry of activity and American status symbol that some call busyness. A friend and I have been collaborating recently on a project that we both recognized wouldn't have been possible for us a few years ago because we were "busy." Asking her what she would have been busy doing, she said, "Absolutely nothing that mattered." We spent the next five minutes laughing at our previous insanity and relieved to find ourselves on the other side. There's a reason that ascetics retreat from the world in search of peace or communion with God and themselves. Recently, we've witnessed a desire for a change in how today's Americans operate. "How to Unplug," manage a "Digital Detox," enjoy a "Sunday Reset," and hold on to the newly discovered leisure time that pandemic office closures forced upon many of the corporate-busy even if not for those classified as essential workers (grocers, medical professionals, mechanics, crafts and tradespeople, warehouse and delivery workers, teachers and other youth workers, etc.). We got a taste for life without aggressive busyness to signal our worth. Of course, things are beginning to revert, but many are keeping the quest for more family time, me time, and time to just *be* at the forefront of their lives.

My friend and I know all too well that the best way not to do what one is called to do is to stay busy doing *absolutely nothing that matters*. Promiscuous activity is any activity not aligned with our sacred duties — to family, community, God, country, and the common good. All of us are, to some extent, guilty of this. Importantly, being unbusy doesn't imply doing nothing but learning to do the right things. Mental solemnity and emotional poise prove constructive for intuiting and extrapolating the ideas most needed to restore and regenerate our world. Learning to ignore life's many allures mercilessly inundating our daily lives and easily accessible through modern technologies is no easy task. To serve effectively, however, we must experience a turning away as a growing urge that immunizes us from life's hustle and bustle just long enough to discover our rightful task and those alongside whom we might best serve.

An important distinction exists between instinct and intuition, often used interchangeably. Instinct refers to a gut reaction or feeling based on a physical or emotional sensitivity to our external environment. Developing the intellect becomes how we learn to control instinctive reactions to avoid pain and suffering and later through self-directed choices that respond to our values, whatever these may be. Therefore, we learn to *think* and dominate our lower nature, irradiating and dissipating our self-created miasmas, hindering proper recognition of *the Good*. Intuition, on the other hand, is a higher sensitivity occurring due to an unfolding subjective awareness and not, therefore, arising from the external environment. Intuition makes us aware of *the Good*, and others who, like us, are becoming perceptive to *the Good* and clear-sighted in its implementation for the whole.

Imagination is the lowest aspect of intuition or this sixth sense. When impulsed by selfish desires, our imaginations distort perceptions of *the Good*, which the intuition transmits to our higher mind. Controlling and clearing away the gross constructions of the American imagination paves the way for those seeking *the Good* to more readily grasp some aspect of it that they can, in collaboration with others similarly focused, implement to improve world conditions. Effectuating the rapid and definite realization of *the Good* is a group effort for all humanitarians and spiritually focused people. Personal desires and fanciful visions of peace, oneness, and unity (because without adequate strength or striving) pollute our shared imagination and must be cleared through self-discipline, reorienting our thoughts to the common good and giving our all in service to it. To benefit the common good means re-*imagining* service as the aim of success and self-mastery as the freely chosen response to the innate call to serve.

Dissipating the miasmas hindering our individual and collective correct perception and interpretation of *the Good* culminates in service. Disciplining and purifying our lower self-serving nature halts our natural tendency to receive and manipulate *the Good* to elevate ourselves or those with whom we've selfishly aligned. The evolutionary Plan unfolding upon our planet persists. It is the perfected and absolute Purpose of God or that creative *Intelligence*, Einstein's *Stupendous Reason*, adapted through Love (understanding and compassion), manifesting Itself more perfectly through humanity as the decades and millennia pass. Consequently, service becomes a reflexive response as people become conscious of and identify themselves with *the Good*. When people begin reorienting from personal self-assertiveness to selfless service, the repose of the higher Self, cooperation and sharing are normalized. In repudiating the goal to assert our capabilities, positions, and influence, we develop the capacity to affirm the group ideal, to use the skills previously used to further our own agendas — good and bad, high and low — to help the group and its members reach its shared goal.

When individuals, groups, organizations, and institutions throughout the nation and world learn to work this way, the possibility of transformation is apparent. No longer will personalities, through violence, deception, manipulation, or charisma, demand conformity to their ideal as the solution to our problems. Instead, we will recognize the true servers and common good leaders as those who inspire others among whom they find themselves with the vision of *the Good*. Their leadership, based on the will-*to-Good*, inaugurates goodwill activities. Increasingly, they are relied upon not as the answer to our problems but as the ones who enable us to find solutions and work together to materialize the new ideals we begin to grasp. Common good leaders radiate and attract people to *the Good*. Rather than demanding compliance with their vision, however beautiful, they demonstrate the integrity of *the Good* by becoming the foremost channels through which it works upon the minds and hearts of others, inviting people to share in its abundance for all. Common good leaders are service-minded leaders whose commitment to the public good supplants their desire for personal gain and, through self-restraint, learn to deliver focused and directed service, becoming enlightened leaders increasingly capable of recognizing and meeting today's local, national, and world challenges. Just as ruggedly individual leaders, often selfish, divisive, ignoble, and willing to win at all costs, appeal to our worst instincts, the selfless and cooperative intent and demonstrated activities of common good leaders can bring out our best. These leaders, who are US!, by reorienting themselves from invigorating the personality to seek the common good, can help build a new nation based on establishing right relations among people, nations, and our shared planetary life.

Midway between the absolute or God and man lies the common good. Between our infinite intellectual capacity to dissect and divide and our eventual identification with the whole lies a subjective impulse, serving to unify humanity as the futility of division and endless differentiation is grasped, leading to new relationships oriented and incentivized by *the Good*. We begin, then, to tread the Way back to unity. Our minds now think from the whole to the part. We envision the starting point as Creation, seeing ourselves as a part of this unfathomable whole. A Return to Unity reorganizes people into new groups and affinities according to a shared purpose to beautify the world based on the universal creative purpose qualified by Love that is *the Good*, reshaping our world according to higher spiritual realities. Willing *the Good* can reorient people from individualistic to cooperative relations, forming the basis for accelerating world restoration and eventual unity.

5.

RIGHT RELATIONS

MY UNCLE MENTIONED being inundated with robocalls from telemarketers. He still uses a flip phone, which should give some indication of his technological prowess. He keeps threatening to get himself a *"what do you call that?"* — smartphone, which would likely require me to hire him an assistant so he could do such things as answer a call, take a picture and text it, save my number in his contacts... things many of us take for granted.

After hearing about the unceasing calls from telemarketers, I lurched into action, adding his cell number to the national and state do-not-call registries. Informing him of this, I told him to give it thirty days or so and let me know if the calls had diminished. Fast forward a year later, he mentions that he's getting even more calls now than before. A few follow-up questions reveal that he has been answering the calls (I had forbidden him from doing this!), saying,

"I figured if I wasted enough of their time by even asking to speak to their supervisor, they would stop calling me." Alas, I fear not. I explained that telemarketers are encouraged by contact — good or bad — not discouraged!

We had been working at cross purposes. As I was working to end contact, he was feeding it. I realized this as a dance the two of us have been in all my life and one that might clarify the two types of workers we can count on to help move our nation forward.

My uncle is attached and inclusive. Now retired, he taught physical education for over forty years alongside managing various community centers within Nashville's Department of Parks and Recreation. He is beloved. I have never met anyone with anything remotely negative to say about him.

We are different.

I am detached and *now* inclusive, but in a different way. Where my uncle always has time for people, even the telemarketers selling something he is most definitely uninterested in buying, I am more discriminating. We agree on unity, inclusive of all people and nations, even as we approach it differently. We have learned much from understanding how the other works. Similarly, our nation's moral exemplars, humanitarians, and people of goodwill who recognize humanity's interrelatedness and interdependence can learn to work together more cohesively when the attached learn to detach while remaining inclusive and the detached become inclusive but not attached.

For *the Attached*, like my uncle, detachment produces the necessary discrimination that enables them to discover the people and groups to which duty and destiny have related them, allowing them to serve most effectively. They must overcome the fear of not being adequately understood or loved. We sometimes call such people "people-pleasers," minimizing their unique capacity to include all. They always find time for others, including some people others think they should have let go long ago. They suffer profusely amidst the divisiveness, fragmentation, and ease at which the digital world inundates us with vitriol. One of the most exacting lessons for true servers is to recognize what is and what is not ours to do. Everywhere we look, we see a need to which we often desperately want to respond. But it is equally true that we cannot do all the things and must strive to discern and undertake the responsibilities that are by virtue of time and place ours to address.

As for *the Detached*, inclusiveness of others' thoughts, ideas, and (God help me) *feelings* produces a proper sense of proportion that enables accurate perception and a willingness to serve the people and groups to whom destiny links them. Pride often prevents *the Detached* from admitting the world's sufferings into their consciousness as a burden to be responsibly shared. They (we) tend towards isolation. Interestingly, the ability to stand alone, indicating leadership, courage, and fearlessness, is the unique gift borne by these servers. Their impetus to "fix" the world drives us toward betterment, but they must learn that it is not theirs alone to do. When, instead of becoming mired in the weeds, *the Detached* learn to create the conditions that swell *the Attached's* ability to draw to the group all that is needed in terms of people, money, and other resources to meet the need, the group's ability to serve humanity increases exponentially.

Growing up in an extended family household included my grandmother and her youngest two children — my mom and uncle. After my grandfather's death, we eventually moved from the church parsonage to a more suburban neighborhood. At the time, few black families were living there. Our neighbors were all white. One of our neighbors pointed a rifle at me one day when two of my older male cousins and I were walking to the store, screaming for me to get out of his yard. For those unaware, due to the lack of sidewalks in residential areas in many parts of the south, it was customary to instruct children to walk along the edge of yards to avoid traffic safely. I may have been around the age of seven when this incident occurred. My cousins walked in the street to my left, safeguarding me from one threat, albeit unknowingly exposing me to another. I was nonplussed and only remember one of the cousins gently and without alarm reaching up to pull me off the yard's edge onto the asphalt alongside them. We successfully reached the store and returned home with whatever snacks we had risked our lives to buy.

If my family ever knew about this, I can't say. They didn't hear it from me. And it's not likely that the cousins shared it because I don't remember any confrontations or police sightings. We simply continued on with life. They were our neighbors for the next twenty or so years. When my grandmother did yard work on Saturday mornings, I'd see her breezily chatting with *The Rifleman's* wife. His young adult children, who appeared to be in their late teens or early twenties, came and went, driving fast cars, dating, and living carefree lives. On occasion, my uncle — *Mr. Attached* — and I would head out or return home together when *The Rifleman* was doing the same. If we were returning home, I'd leap out of the car and barrel towards the house as soon as the car came to a slow roll. Sometimes, halted midair, I'd hear what had become a familiar exchange.

Uncle: "*Good morning.*"

The Rifleman: Dead silence.

Uncle: "*I said, Good morning!*" he intoned as righteously threatening as it was pleasant.

The Rifleman: "*Mumble...mumble...,*" said grimacing. Pleasantries were exchanged, and both men returned to their activities and separate lives.

I always wondered why my uncle insisted on these exchanges.

Why waste time talking to him? I, *Ms. Detached*, never bothered to know the names of this family. I lived as carefree a life as I had observed their children living. I graduated high school, left for college, visited home, and then one day, they were gone. There had been other incidents throughout my early teens. No guns. But their two Great Danes gave chase (I learned how to climb trees fast) until I realized they were trained only to go so far.

Some people will wonder how I could be so nonchalant about this experience. The truth is that, on some level, I knew that I was a child of God. I was in touch with the part of me — the soul — that could not be touched by *The Rifleman's* ignorance or hatred. I knew that he could *kill* me. But he could not *touch* me. The divine me. The immortal me. The me that is an indissoluble part of the Whole. Unlike my uncle, I didn't always so easily recognize the divine in others. I didn't *love* them any less, but I wasn't going out of my way to win over their souls either. I loved humanity even if I didn't necessarily always like *humans*.

It was only much later in life that I understood that my uncle's insistence to evoke a returned pleasantry wasn't for his benefit but to help our neighbor encounter his better angels. His attachment to people, even those we might deem undeserving, made it possible for him to help them see in themselves what he already saw in them — their imperfect humanity and their unrealized divinity. It is not an easy lesson for *the Detached* to learn, impervious as we are to the messiness of others' "stuff." When we let others in, we often discover that we are equipped to aid them not by solving their problems but by giving them the strength to tell the telemarketers to add their names to the do-not-call lists without even so much as a *please* and *thank you*.

Re-entering the classroom tested and perfected my ability to be detached and inclusive. To best serve students whose lives were often challenging and sometimes just downright unlucky amplified the need to speak life into them, which occasionally sounded harsh to listeners persuaded that circumstances define us. Others, unaware or unconvinced of the divine within each of us, cannot provide the necessary spark to light this inner fire. Instead, we often see teachers, parents, and other caring adults further entrench a sense of helplessness among youth who most need strength, fortitude, and hope. I acknowledged the students' difficulties. But I refused to allow them to define themselves by their trauma!

Seeing and cultivating children's awareness of the divine aspect within them was the only solid foundation upon which I knew I could help them discover a suitable vocation, draw out the best within them, and eventually choose willingly and consciously to serve the whole because they know themselves to be an integral part of it. None of this negates that Americans must do better for the oppressed, vulnerable, and strivers. But in the meantime (which this book intends to condense dramatically) ...Through contact with the soul within, we can — individually and collectively — solve all problems, find those who can help us and whom we can help, pierce through the illusion of separateness, revealing the unity of all. I knew that divinity was within me, and there was no way anything, anyone, or any circumstance would stop it from unleashing its good.

The approach I outline is distinctly non-material, albeit capable of radically transforming material circumstances. The combined efforts of the *Attached* and the *Detached* are needed to carry it out. *The Attached* are, too often, focused on alleviating others' pain as it reminds them of their discomfort. *The Detached*, however, can bear the discomfort but usually choose not to intervene. The former focuses too stridently on assuaging the demands of the form (personality), which naturally insists on creature comforts, and the latter too quickly dismisses people's rightful need for relief.

The issue, however, in national and world events is the result of our emphasis on material outcomes without due attention paid to spiritual causes. The seemingly new programs, practices, and thought leadership are too often well-meaning manipulations of existing ideals whose time has passed. Breakthroughs are, by definition, outside the realm of present practices. They impose a depth and breadth of vision, expanding possibilities that serve, absent interference from our personal and, therefore, self-serving desires, the good of the whole. The work of the soul upon our minds enlightens, which simply means it brings light to the dark places within us and our environment, enabling us to escape from all that diminishes contact with our divinity. When contact is made and sustained, we know ourselves to be in the world but not of the world. Then will the soul control the outer form and life and all events. Material circumstances of either a positive or negative kind can, then, be interpreted and handled per the soul's objectives, which in every case are group awareness, group service, and group progress. When viewing the fissures in present-day ideals and institutions, we can ask what new forms the soul seeks to build of greater benefit to us individually and collectively. Rather than prop up that which has served us for better or worse, the soul asks that we release what has been and, under its direction, build anew.

Change is typically easier and relished by *the Detached* and avoided by *the Attached*, indicating the need for these types to work together to build a new civilization and culture with greater facility while guarding against undue harm, especially to those most fearful and bewildered by today's rapid changes. *The Attached* are the people in organizations speaking in measured pronouncements, hesitating to rush to conclusions or take action, and asking lots and lots of clarifying questions. They don't always agree that "done is better than perfect," especially when making decisions that can potentially create even more significant harm. *The Attached* can't help but concern themselves with how others might be affected by the group's actions. *Before* becoming inclusive, *the Detached* want *the Attached* to hurry along, focusing only on the thrill of revolutionary change despite its potential for destroying livelihoods, communities, and overall well-being. *The Detached* want to "move fast and break things," and, lacking an inclusive vision, they fail to see or be deterred by the landmines obvious to *the Attached*. Frustration exists on both ends: *the Attached* can't believe that, yet again, *the Detached* are building and launching the next new thing, ignoring the numerous red flags brought up in reports and meetings. *The Detached* think *the Attached* worry too much and that whatever bad happens will be minimal compared to the [g]ood that results. Each type may grasp some aspect of *the Good*. Still, cooperation remains imperative until humanity demonstrates that higher reason we call intuition, bypassing altogether the lower self, its reactions, desires, and aspirations. The personality analyzes. The soul *knows*; it reasons from the universal to the particular and is, therefore, capable of creating new possibilities that carry within them what is good for the whole.

These two types — *the Attached* and *the Detached* — exist within all institutions and, after learning to work cooperatively, can solve all of our problems, presenting those unifying, synthesizing, and adaptive ideas that meet the needs of the common good. Both approaches are needed. Sometimes, it is necessary to cut our losses, as *the Detached* (who do love humanity!) know, but it is equally valid, as *the Attached* know, that the cut-off point is often not where *the Detached* have so quickly drawn it. Blending the two ways helps to achieve right relationships, right responsibility, and right service, permitting *the Good* to reach even the darkest crevices of our nation and world, enlightening our minds, steering our thoughts, and inspiring practical goodwill actions. Being receptive and impressed by *the Good* helps us create a new nation made by and for the good of the whole.

Right relations between and among people, nations, and the varied planetary lives develop neither from coercion nor rationality. The former would impose Brotherhood, undermining the unifying and synthesizing integrity of *the Good* and invalidating humanity's freedom to choose or reject it. On the other hand, rationality, the separating and differentiating faculty of the intellect, requires the aid of the group conscious higher Self to recognize our interrelatedness. The nature of the unenlightened personality is separative, whereas the enlightened personality, aware of its group relations, is universal. Clinging too tightly to our individuality prevents us from embracing the common good. The solution, however, cannot be achieved by mandate, absolving each of self-selected responsibility to the whole and retarding their advancement towards realizing the part that is theirs to play.

The common good dawns most easily upon our minds through exposure to the effects of *the Good*. Incentivized by the will-*to-Good*, we create and manifest *the Good*, attracting, nourishing, and sustaining goodwill and right relations from and among all. Proliferating *the Good* throughout society at every level is the best way to attract and awaken others to its possibilities that, in due time, elicit each human being's voluntary participation to manifest the common good as they see fit. Right relations is a willed intent to take responsibility for as much of today's challenges as we can bear based on our understanding of world issues and a recognized ability to address them. Right relations combine universality, connecting each to all and love for humanity, focusing and directing our thoughts and capabilities to realize the greatest good for the greatest number.

Common good leaders, by their thoughts, words, and actions,

prove the validity of *the Good*. Unlike the deceptive and manipulative practices often used by rugged individualists, true world servers reject coercive "successes" because they infantilize and weaken others' will and deny the divinity of each person. Common good leaders understand that short-term success gained at the expense of free will delays development, obscuring each person's more refined and group-oriented nature, and, as a result, prevents others from true participation in *the Good*. Cooperative individualism demands truth, transparency, and an immovable faith that the spiritual self, discovered by some, also exists within every person, organization, institution, and nation. Our primary responsibility then transforms from getting people to do what we want and believe what we believe to living and being *the Good*, allowing it to work upon the hearts and minds of others through us. This reliance upon and subsequent nurturing of people's realization of *the Good* is the foundation of right relations. There is an assumed subjective unity even while recognizing a vast objective differentiation among people and cultures.

When teaching, I was often reminded that schools are a microcosm of the larger society. Whatever insanity occurs "out there" will most certainly spill into the school environment. The many programs — service-learning, civics and leadership, bullying prevention, social-emotional learning, trauma-informed care, etc. — strive, in some measure, to make children and the schools they attend somehow different from the larger society in which they exist. Despite a measure of success, no school program can adequately offset the harms caused by our collective lack of right relations. These programs inevitably create more demands upon teachers and school administrators. Inundated with a constant stream of programming to make children be better than us, teachers and students are overwhelmed, and students are no better. Right relations are everyone's responsibility — teachers, children, parents, government, neighbors, businesses, religious leaders, and so on.

When we are collectively better, schools and children will be better. If I made students better during their time with me, it was because I recognized the good in them often despite their shenanigans. I was not an easy teacher. I was unequivocal in my expectations. Only when a student voluntarily undertook such responsibilities as wiping down the chalkboard or desks, vacuuming, and picking up the occasional trash left behind could they have a say in how I ran the classroom, which they never did. It was a shared space, yes. But the classroom operated according to my wisdom, not students' self-aggrandizing dogmatism, exacting harsh consequences for everyone but themselves and their closest friends who changed daily if not on the hour. Students understood that while I valued them as equals, recognizing our commonality as expressions of divinity, I also assumed responsibility for each of them and the entire classroom. They entrusted me with greater responsibility without demand or force due to a persistent demonstration of loving understanding, wise actions, and self-initiated restoration when I failed to uphold these standards in relationship to them.

My only rule was to strive to be your best self. When students — and they always did — stepped out of line, they could count on me to talk them through it. Students understood that they could disagree with me, argue with me, insist on their right to mistreat others, try their best to prove why another student didn't deserve respect or compassion, and yet remain in good favor with me. Detached and inclusive, I ultimately wore them down by letting *the Good* do its work. I didn't demand that they do good. I tried to be good instead. I didn't insist that they treat others fairly. Instead, I was persistently just and fair with everyone at all times. I believed in the good in each student, and my conviction convinced them to believe in it, too. Many, if not most, teachers would prefer to teach the next generations in this way. Some manage to do so despite the many bureaucratic obstacles pulling them this way or that. Most would agree that we don't need new or better programs to improve students but better people in their homes, communities, their parents' workplaces, and serving politically at the local, state, and national levels. The children are okay unless and until we make them not okay! It is we who must believe in our good and see to it that we let it shine forth.

I was very intentional in creating a hierarchy of goodwill in my classroom. Achieving this required persistent attention to *universality, love for humanity*, and *self-restraint*.

Intent on considering and serving the needs of students, other teachers, the larger campus community, and the families and communities into which we would release them after graduation evoked the will-*to-Good* based on a more inclusive vision than what might have been most expedient for me. I had many "come to Jesus" talks with students about issues that arose in their cottages, relationships with their parents and other students or adults on campus, and, of course, within themselves, which hindered their progress as students and human beings. The more widespread my concern for children as part of a greater whole, the more access I had to inspired ideas, which helped to address immediate concerns in ways that equally supported long-term and collective well-being. Striving to understand the needs of the whole coupled with a love for the child was paramount to bridging the gap between doing what was good for the child and humanity as a whole. For each of us attempting to serve humanity and the world, it should become increasingly impossible to surrender the common good to the whims of an individual or attempt to achieve unity by forsaking, casting off, or wantonly sacrificing a person or group.

Outside of the occasional physical altercation where students needed to be separated, I asked only one student to leave the classroom during three years of teaching. When we met later, I expressed regret for sending him to the office, explaining that it was a last resort. I told him that it's not my practice to ask students to leave the class because it is a loss for them in terms of missing out on what we are learning, but it is also a loss for the classroom as a whole. His peers and I miss out on what he offers to the class. At the same time, I made it clear to him that his behavior was inappropriate and could not continue. Then, I asked for his help in finding a way for him to return to and stay in class, supporting our shared goal of learning, growth, and mutual enjoyment. Over the next couple of weeks, he made improvements. Nevertheless, we experienced moments of continued misbehaving, which quick sidebars and reminders alleviated for the most part.

A few weeks later, we were reading the play *Twelve Angry Men*. Reading the play aloud, students took on roles each day. One day, I asked this student to read aloud the part of Juror Three, the play's primary antagonist. Lee J. Cobb brilliantly plays him in the 1957 film, which we later watched. He speaks a lot in the play and is boisterous and vehement about his desire to see the teenager on trial convicted for killing his father. Taking on this role, our previously disruptive student became a star! His enthusiasm brought this character to life, replete with this jurors' anger, pain, and regret. He was not the most well-liked kid, but the entire class rallied around him that day. They applauded his masterful performance, telling him how great it was. After that day, students refused to allow anyone else to read Juror Three's part. At least for a brief moment, the student could experience a wellspring of goodwill towards him due to his self-restraint and willing positive contribution to our classroom. From then on, he became a model student: always prepared for class, asking for and receiving help when needed, helping other students when he could without being asked, and being pleasant to be around.

When making an effort to become a channel for *the Good* to work upon the hearts and minds of others, irrespective of age or ability, the people we come into contact with can and will develop along lines that permit them to a greater or lesser degree to conform their thoughts and actions to *the Good*. I was never willing to sacrifice one poorly behaving student through expulsion from the classroom or school, and the same must be valid for society as a whole. Prisons are full of former misbehaving students whose sense of being disposable helped shape them into recalcitrant and anti-social adults. It would be foolish to say simply that the solution can be found in some sentimental, loving attitude towards them. Instead, we must embody the love inspired by the will-*to-Good* and translate it into practical and intelligent actions in classrooms, homes, workplaces, communities, governments, and nations that create the right relationships, policies, and systems to serve the ultimate good of the individual, group, and whole.

When we avert our responsibility to integrate the individual into the larger whole, casting aside those we deem irredeemable or unworthy, we entrench anti-social behaviors and prolong our collective suffering through attempts to unify a whole while, at the same time, cutting some off from it. There is one *Life* of which each of us is an indissoluble part. Our aim must be to awaken all people we contact to the reality of our essential unity.

The expressed will-*to-Good* that will usher in the practical living that lifts humanity to betterment awakens the individual's will-to-serve, transforming personal desire and aspiration from essentially self-serving pursuits to collective benefit. People then aspire to the roles and work that match their skills and interests but are also inextricably tied to the needs of their community, nation, or world.

As the will-*to-Good* spreads, it gives rise to an intelligent public goodwill, affirming a natural rather than imposed hierarchy (or order). It is a hierarchy similar to the one my students eventually yielded to through recognition and voluntary sacrifice of their personal (and often self-serving) desires and aspirations rather than through coercion or coaxing. Students, desirous of harmonizing with *the Good*, demanded more of it from themselves and their peers, caretakers, and families. In this way, *the Good* is self-reinforcing. Once people experience it, they begin to crave more of it, be inspired by it, conform to it, and cultivate it in their relations with others. We can see how a little *Good* can go a long way. Eventually, all people will demand selfless leaders, effective stewardship, and an education that prepares each person to fulfill their role in society, calling forth the best in each of us. Then humanity, generations hence, will have arrived at a time when there is a widespread consciousness of the common good, replacing all self-serving thoughts of *me*, *my* and *mine*, and where only the greatest good for the greatest number captures our attention and imagination.

6.

LOVE THY NEIGHBOR

SINCE ITS FOUNDING, America has had a diverse religious landscape. Even its largest religion, Christianity, has a varied tapestry, which includes evangelicals, protestants, Catholics, Mormons, and others. Although there is disagreement about whether or not the U.S. is a Christian nation, at roughly 64% of the population (and falling), according to the Pew Research Center,[10] it's hard to argue that Christianity hasn't had, perhaps, an outsize influence on the nation through its followers. Some years ago, one pastor wrote concerning the state of our nation that many of us are church members but not yet Christians.

---

10   NW, 1615 L. St, et al. "Modeling the Future of Religion in America." *Pew Research Center's Religion & Public Life Project*, 13 September 2022, www. pewresearch.org/religion/2022/09/13/modeling-the-future-of-religion-in-america/#:~:text=The%20Center%20estimates%20that%20in.

Ponder on this.

Love, most agree, most aptly and succinctly personifies Christ's life and message. When asked to articulate the great commandment in the law, the Master Jesus responded, saying, "Thou shalt love the Lord thy God with all thy heart, and with all thy soul, and with all thy mind. This is the first and great commandment. And the second is like unto it, Thou shalt love thy neighbor as thyself. On these two commandments hang all the law and the prophets." Matthew 22:37-40 At its simplest, the Teachings indicate that a person embodies the spirit of Christ when they demonstrate a love for the whole (God) and the part (neighbor/Commons) factually. The Common Good includes the totality of lives — spiritual, human, and nonhuman — that make up the life of our planet. To the Christian, loving God must mean the same as it does to the agnostic or the atheist who has some sense of the universality of *life*. God is the whole of which we each are a part. To love God, then, and not love the parts may qualify one as "church," but it fails to make one Christian.

God is Love (1 John 4:16) describes His nature and indicates the motivating impulse behind Creation. Love manifests as *the Good*, imprinting God's pattern upon an evolving Creation so that we might consciously share in Its beautification. Whatever impedes our recognition of *the Good* prevents the free flow of the renewing source of the will-*to-Good* into and throughout the planet. When individuals and groups can correctly invoke, correctly interpret and apply the pattern or Plan that is *the Good* through skill-in-action, we can better address all human and environmental challenges in service to the common good. Making the world better, then, insists on an accurate perception of *the Good* and love for the whole and the part, love for God and the Commons. Only this combination permits us to do our rightful part.

The true Christian includes all who recognize themselves as an integral part of the vast and greater whole and develop themselves to increase their capacity to serve the whole. Christ's sacrifice foretells the opportunity for each to sacrifice for the nation's common good and, eventually, for each nation to restore the world through its sacrifice to the whole. The many world crises faced today provide the friction necessary to enlarge every nation's capacity to recognize that we're all in this together, and in due time, each must set aside its nationalism, which too often breeds selfishness and a sense of superiority among its citizens, and also adopt a shared vision, benefitting the common good.

As *the Good* incentivizes more leaders, irrespective of their social, political, religious, or national affiliations, they will see clearly humanity's needs and create the solutions to meet them. Such leaders do not selfishly aspire to power but selflessly seek to equip themselves to steward resources to benefit the whole, according to a continuum of demonstrated right responsibility.

Our aim must include identifying, developing, and mobilizing selfless leaders committed to and capable of effective trusteeship, coupled with a system of education that prepares each person to fulfill their role in society, calling forth the best in each of us. Then, we can be assured that future leaders and those who must, as yet, still be led will take up their rightful positions within society willingly, reverentially, and with a mutual commitment to the common good.

Fulfilling *the Good* occurs when it correctly leads individuals, groups, and nations to understand and cooperate to achieve greater unity, inspiring and creating goodwill for and among all. Encouraging our nation's leaders to channel their ambitions and aspirations toward broader societal welfare fosters a culture of selflessness and cooperation. This shift in perspective can reshape institutions from within, infusing them with renewed purpose and relevance. Once more, we can take up the ideal pronounced in the

Four Freedoms (1941) (the freedom of speech, the freedom of worship, the freedom from want, and the freedom from fear) based on a recognition that only true freedom of choice allows people to *consciously* and *willingly* choose spiritual values over materialistic ideals, identifying themselves increasingly with *the Good*. Individually interpreted with reverence rather than indulgence, these freedoms can provide a new basis for building a new nation and world.

Prone to personality distortions, humanity misconstrues freedom as license. The corrective, leading to liberation from our attachments to forms and thus capable of accurate perception of the one essential *Life*, which is humanity's right and destiny, is only accessible through sustained contact with *the Good*. Christ recognized the One Life (God). Further, he understood that each human being (a son of God) carried within them the seed of universality that, when realized, would make each aware of and dedicated to the good of the whole or the common good. Loving thy neighbor demonstrates that one is becoming universal in one's consciousness, notwithstanding one's individuality and recognition of the diversity of appearances. Our neighbors include spiritual Beings, such as the Buddha and the Christ, others having ascended above the vagaries of human experience yet still sharing in our sufferings and guiding us ever forward, and the nonhuman kingdoms for which humanity must inevitably accept responsibility.

When we submit to *the Good*, we find communion among all Creation. We, then, discover, like Whitman, that we contain multitudes within. Realizing our universality (as souls), we undertake the necessary purification imposed by the light that is *the Good*, magnetizing and attracting us into a deeper relationship with it and, therefore, right relations with all human beings and our planetary life. Eventually, we become enlightened personalities, transfigured (as were Buddha and Christ) by *the Good*. All who partake in furthering *the Good* for the common good embody the Christ consciousness, irrespective of their religion, agnosticism, or atheism.

To be Christian must be understood beyond what it means to be "church." His life testified to the realizable fusion between personality and soul, spirit and matter, indicating a new possibility for humanity and demonstrating the stupendousness of its fruition. All people may call themselves Christians who invoke *the Good* to serve the common good. Refusing this, even when rapt with devotion to God, one cannot call oneself Christian but merely a church member.

7.

WILLING "THE GOOD"

GOODWILL AMONG PEOPLE is evident among all races, classes, religions, political groups, and nations. Grassroots efforts to replace competition with cooperation and hoarding with sharing appear everywhere. However, we lack the coordinated efforts of those writers, artists, politicians, religious leaders, scientists, business executives, and skilled workers who conceive of ideas capable of remedying the harms — individual and collective, national and global — caused by human selfishness. People who have some grasp of *the Good* and spiritual-minded people have obviated their duty and responsibility, allowing the more individualistic or selfish individuals to lead. A deliberate assumption of sharing and cooperation must exist to alleviate suffering and renew a commitment to the common good.

Collectively, we've used the power of creative imagination to attach ourselves to high and low desires, tethering us to fitful cycles of having and not-having, wanting and not wanting, desiring and rejecting. Our collective selfishness, hatred, separateness, and low ambitions hang overhead, darkening the way forward. And can only be overcome by the will-*to-Good*, which is *Love*. Will relinquishes desire. Will aligns all thoughts, speech, and activities with divine Purpose. Specifically, demonstrating the will-*to-Good* by becoming receptive to the Plan that is unfolding upon our planet, expressing a more perfect beauty, truth, and goodness, and striving to rightly interpret and manifest it for the common good quenches the fires of desire and transfigures high aspirations into realized purpose. Leaders willing to sacrifice their desires and aspirations to participate in *the Good* can make a coordinated impact in all fields of human endeavor, amplifying the public's goodwill to create practical solutions to our most challenging problems. This cross-sector coordinated activity in service to the greatest good for the greatest number will give birth to a new world based on right relations between and among people, nations, and the planet.

Rebuilding requires balancing the outgoing ways of life with the incoming possibilities, carefully preserving what is essential and releasing what is nonessential. Universality, love for humanity, and self-restraint are the three tendencies evinced by decision-makers capable of helping us navigate and ease the pains of transition from the old ways of life to the more flourishing life humanity demands. Likewise, all people seeking to increase their capacity to serve during this historic cultural shift from a nation governed by *selfish* personalities to one guided by more *selfless* souls can use these qualities as a guidepost.

Universality indicates recognition of the interconnectedness of our planet's people, nations, and all life. A universal sense deliberately includes, motivating identification. Individual, group, and national contributions and distress are equally acknowledged, leading to the equitable distribution of resources among people and nations according to need. Universality differs from multiculturalism or internationalism, although it includes these. We experience true universality as an immediate shattering of the protective shell of individuality, unmasking our relation to the whole. We feel that we are everything all at once. Although identification is instantaneous, the time it takes to achieve a realized synthesis with all that is must be won through daily living and learning to serve the good of the whole. Recognizing that one's capacity to invoke *the Good* demands its rightful circulation for the common good, which includes all human and planetary life, makes the will-*to-Good* operable.

Love for Humanity encourages us to develop our unique skills and capabilities to benefit a shared purpose based upon goodwill to all. This love is not sentimental. Neither is it a theoretical feeling of oneness. It acknowledges a fundamental unity and Brotherhood that enables us to develop ourselves to serve all. Appropriate perception of *the Good* and intelligently working it out based on present possibilities rather than categorical adherence to fixed ideas about how things should or shouldn't be indicate love for humanity through demonstrated compassion and understanding. Love for others always provokes the need to hold fast to the vision of *the Good* encountered, adapting it based on wise discernment for people's present ability to realize it. To be effective requires that we temper idealism with clearsightedness. We become optimistic realists, holding fast to the vision and, at the same time, dealing practically with things as they are. In this way, humanity is led from goal to goal with steadfastness to reach ever nearer perfection.

Self-restraint helps us voluntarily focus and direct our ambitions and aspirations for the common good rather than personal gain. We learn to abstain from self-interested assertion to secure a greater good for others. Striving to realize a shared purpose requires us to voluntarily give up our cherished ideas, attachments, methods of working, and anything else that might stand in the way of the goal. Participating in such an endeavor cultivates a willingness to sacrifice that doesn't necessitate suffering because it is a voluntary choice and increasingly becomes a reflexive response, fulfilling a shared ideal that takes the place of otherwise individualistic achievement.

Motivation to actualize these qualities — universality, love for humanity, and self-restraint — helps us build and consolidate efforts across many sectors of human living, forging a unity of purpose and igniting synchronistic yet multifaceted priorities and approaches to ensure widespread impact at every level. Felt relief among the public due to the organized, focused, and directed will-*to-Good* among humanitarian and spiritually-oriented individuals and groups creates a collective, successful counter to the selfishly-oriented wills of the people and groups still, by and large, ruggedly individual. Maintaining a posture of universality, love for humanity, and self-restraint, we help increase the capacity and determination of the many people of goodwill. When impulsed by the will-*to-Good* to intuit ideas, create practical ideals, and take action to serve the whole, we affirm *the Good* through our efforts and make it a reality for all. Further, striving to embody these qualities produces a capacity for mutual and instantaneous recognition of others sharing a similarity of vision and objective, revealing an opportunity to cooperate or otherwise assist each other's efforts to which all are interested and committed. These subjective alliances become the basis of the needed group endeavors capable of generating rapid results to transform present conditions.

For too long, we have interpreted Christ's teachings about love according to a selfish, individualistic consciousness, equating it with sentimentality, jealousy, possession, something finite, separating, and exclusionary. Distorting love in this way reinforced our separation and undermined our ability to realize the breadth and depth of the power of love. Love is impersonal because it is limitless and universal, indicating its equal application to all life. When released from largely self-serving motivations, love can be used for good. In reality, to love is to be in the right relationship with life or Creation: human, subhuman, planetary, or cosmic. Love is reason, transcendent and immanent. Einstein's "stupendous reason" — God — is that *Great* and *Transcendent Good* lying behind Creation, and immanent, found at the heart of each atom — human, solar, and cosmic — which still has more to teach us. Love interprets God's Purpose and conditions the unfolding Plan upon our planet. It's *the Good* awaiting human recognition and nurturing humanity's eventual full participation and creative agency. Love is instantaneous and direct comprehension of truth, made available to those who overcome emotional and mental obstacles preventing correct contact, interpretation, and response based on knowledge of and resonance with *the Good*.

For this reason, love is called *pure reason,* indicating one's ability to arrive at it without the more typical deceptive mental reasoning of our separative and analytical minds. Love is essential before unity. Love is an act of will — the will-*to-Good* — without which power, in human hands, proves unintelligent and destructive. People concerned about solving the problems facing our nation and world, dedicated to the common good, and working selflessly and tirelessly with others to find solutions despite apparent lack of success can more readily contact *the Good* necessary to evoke the will-*to-Good*, thereby ushering in the spread of goodwill, restoring public trust in our institutions and each other.

The New York Times highlighted a study[11] conducted by psychologists during the early days of the pandemic, which found would-be purchasers of first or second firearms "more likely to see the world as dangerous and threatening than individuals who were not planning to purchase a firearm."[12]

> *Those planning to buy firearms were more likely to agree strongly with statements like "People can't be trusted," "People are not what they seem," and "You need to watch your back," compared with those not planning a purchase, noted Dr. Anestis, an author of the study.*
>
> *Buyers were also more fearful of uncertainty. They tended to strongly agree with statements such as "Unforeseen events upset me greatly" and "I don't like not knowing what comes next."* (Rabin)

Taking a "For" or "Against" position on issues articulates the problems of humanity, revealing our most stark cleavages. Yet, finding solutions to contentious issues regarding abortion, guns, climate change, vaccines, and other polarizing issues cannot be solved by further analysis. However, the discriminating mind has clarified demarcations between opposing sides. The middle way (as most eloquently articulated by the Buddha) must then be discovered

---

11   Anestis, M.D. and Bryan, C.J. (2021). Threat perceptions and the intention to acquire firearms. *Journal of Psychiatric Research*, 133, pp.113–118. doi:https://doi.org/10.1016/j.jpsychires.2020.12.033.

12   Rabin, Roni Caryn. "Why Some Americans Buy Guns." *The New York Times*, 23 June 2023, www.nytimes.com/2023/06/23/health/gun-violence-psychology.html.

through the enlightened mind, a mind in touch with *the Good*, capable of holding an unwavering focus that refuses to turn toward one extreme or the other, awaiting the entrance of that which is new, innovative, and capable of bridging between the two poles of opposition. When conditioning our minds, *the Good* cultivates concern for the group's needs based on group identification, group love, group understanding, and group good. Wherever opposing sides exist, we must seek relief through contact with the highest *Good*.

The Good synthesizes the many into the few: individuals into groups, groups into nations, and all into the one humanity and one planet. Instead of seeing humanity in its vast diversity, *the Good* begins to break down the barriers that allow people to see behind outer differences that cause distrust and fear of others and the world, to reveal an essentiality that unites each to all. This position permits us to discover solutions to our most intractable problems and implement them for humanity's welfare. When we say that people are losing faith in each other, institutions, the nation, and the world, we mean that they are losing faith in *the Good*. They don't as readily see the good in others or the world around them. When this persists, humanity has a choice to either will *the Good* or refuse, allowing the vision of *the Good* to atrophy, recede from our memories, and, as a consequence, compel our self-destruction. The choice is ours, collectively, to make.

To be clear, however, even humanity's free will is a temporal construct limited by the Will and Purpose of the greater Life in which it participates. Essentially, free will, leading as it has to non-conformity with the Will of God through either ignorance or recalcitrance, must eventually end. A more deliberate conscious evolution makes the end of suffering possible through self-knowledge, group consciousness, and finally, identity with the one life.

Someday, the people of goodwill across the globe can will into being the unrealized vision for a better world that ends needless suffering, brings peace to all people in all lands, unites rather than divides, distributes the earth's resources equitably and sustainably, brings an end to war and nuclear armaments, and recognizes the common good for all.

The cause of all imperialism, oppression, genocide, the dominance of one race over another, and religious conflicts in human history is the result of separateness and selfishness. In every instance, human beings have sought to carve out a claim on the earth's abundance to secure happiness, tranquility, peace, cultural dominance, riches, and power for themselves and those they love. All are complicit in making the world what it is, acted out equally on the world stage between nations and frequently meted out in the daily interactions among families, neighbors, and strangers. We ameliorate outer conflicts by recognizing them first as externalized expressions of the opposition within us between our lower and higher Selves, our self-centered personality, and our group-conscious soul. As souls, people, organizations, and nations become channels for *the Good,* and by serving *the Good*, they become *the Good*, an outer expression in time and space of as much of *the Great Good* as is possible for each, which is the Will and Purpose of God. Absent a few good Minds willing *the Good*, humanity will repeat fractious cycles between peoples, cultures, religions, and nations with more frequency and less reprieve.

We hold within our hands the power to build the world anew and along more right lines, conforming to *the Good* or choosing to architect our destruction instead. The people who, through self-forgetfulness and harmlessness, can contact *the Good* have a responsibility to ensure its accessibility through practical ideals worked out in every field of human experience that make it impossible for people anywhere upon the earth to doubt *the Good* exists. We must ensure that *the Good* reaches *the highest mountains and flows to the lowest valleys*, spreading goodwill and inculcating right relations among everyone everywhere.

Nevertheless, the will-*to-Good*, executed with the right motive and skilled facility, by common good leaders cannot usurp the people's will. All people have the right to choose or reject *the Good*. Leaders are responsible only for fitting themselves to intuit *the Good* correctly, overcoming the temptations of sought-after ambitions to secure popularity, influence, and power over others that thwart correct interpretation, and responsibly serve others wherever they find themselves with the best that is within them. Living for *the Good* and willing *the Good* teaches us to trust and depend on *the Good.* Discovering the light of *the Good* within ourselves, we become the light, magnetic and attractive to others who seek a way out of darkness, true freedom, and intimacy with *the Good* for themselves. Common good leaders remind humanity of the vision by willing *the Good* through their deliberate sacrifice of personal gain to serve others.

The majority of people are good, I believe. They want for others what they want for themselves: good-paying jobs, safe communities, nurturing families, and access to the resources that help people secure well-being for themselves and those they love. It begs the question: *How do good-natured and well-meaning people nevertheless help incentivize and maintain the status quo?*

The argument often made by some is that existing inequities are outside of their control, preventing them from doing the good they want to do. Companies blame the pipeline for lack of diverse candidates, colleges blame K-12 for lack of rigor, schools blame parents, rich blame the poor, and everyone blames the government. Many leaders genuinely want to diversify their companies and organizations, expand opportunities to students who didn't attend one of the most selective colleges and universities, and stem the transfer of wealth, making the rich richer, the poor poorer, and further decimating the middle class. Understanding what can and must be done is not what they lack. Instead, they lack an appropriate and proportional assumption of responsibility incentivized by the will-*to-Good*. Not only must common good leaders be capable of envisioning and articulating new ideals, but they must also prevent their further misapplication, misdirection, and misuse to maintain the status quo. The history of America is not one doomed by lack of vision but rather an expansive vision often co-opted and engineered to serve the few and not the many. Achieving the greatest good for the greatest number must be the litmus test against which all proposed solutions, activities, and results are persistently vetted by those aiming to manifest *the Good.*

With the entrance of that which is new, which is the will-*to-Good*, we can avoid repeating past mistakes. Instead of using new names for old ideas or rebuilding systems and institutions that more deeply entrench and mask outworn practices while labeling it change, the will-*to-Good* illuminates the need and clarifies the optimal responses. Without the inspired activity of the will-*to-Good*, which is foremost the motivation of the group conscious soul, humanity is doomed to repeat its past perpetually, further distancing us from the light transmitting *the Good.* Only by recognizing the destruction taking place all around us as possibilities — rightly interpreted and confronted by us as aspiring or realized souls — can we factually build back better.

Each of us can attest to feeling the excitement of a new thing or many new things proffered to save the planet, eradicate homelessness, end racism, ameliorate educational and economic inequities, and unify our nation, only to feel more disillusioned when surprise *surprise* such solutions fail, and we find matters even worse. Absent the will-*to-Good*, we lack what is essential for beautifying and harmonizing the world and any part within it, large or small. The difference lies in the intention. We are motivated either by personal desire (largely selfish), a higher personal aspiration, including *some* others but not all, or the will-*to-Good*, dedicated to the whole. Only the latter, focused on group solidarity, group need, and group good, can suffice to build anew all that we have constructed based on self-serving personal or group desires and aspirations, either high, medium, or low. In this way, common good leaders, animated by the will-*to-Good*, spontaneously evoke people's higher spiritual impulses and goodwill, unleashing *the Good* among all and through all.

We dare not leave the task of world betterment to any one person, group, or nation. We who love humanity and seek ever the good of the whole cannot shirk our duty and responsibility, leaving those who don't know or don't see in the hands and under the direction of the selfish, power-obsessed, and greedy. In small and large ways, each of us must strain ourselves to do more to offset the forces aligned against human progress, against human freedom, and against *unleashing the Good.*

8.

PRIORITIZING "THE GOOD"

THE LEGISLATION, POLICIES, and practices imposed by a few
decision-makers throughout every sector of American society,
often punitive and regressive, harm many people's lives. When eval-
uated according to the principle aim of the common good, which
establishes the needed environments to reinforce each person's commitment and contribution to *the Good*, it demands a reorganization
of society to validate all people's indissoluble unity with the whole.
As a result of this new impetus, decision-makers across all fields of
human enterprise take responsibility for establishing those prec-
edents that prepare each person to develop themselves according
to the vision of the Commons that increasingly absorbs them and
takes root in their minds and their hearts, inspiring their striving
and eventual autonomous contribution. Motivated increasingly by
a vision of what can be, prioritizing the common good must begin

to replace present and primarily penalizing practices as more leaders become absorbed into the creative possibilities of *the Good* to inspire positive change among all people and at every stage of development. Then, an enlightened public opinion will rise up to determine those laws that must govern right human relations and choose leaders most equipped to build frameworks for daily living that serve the greatest good for the greatest number.

We can best understand the two primary approaches to human development as either emphasizing behavioral control or, instead, positive reinforcement, which helps others develop their often hidden capacity to think, to understand their relationships to others and the harms they cause, and to choose a more right action of their own volition. In the first instance, modifying behavior may provide short-term results, but often at the expense of helping others master themselves. Punitive measures have neither eradicated nor deterred crime in America. Nor has discipline or shaming engendered more prosocial behaviors among antisocial people. Threats to welfare benefits based on mental health, substance abuse treatment, or work mandates also fail to yield healthier people and societies. It is vision that is needed.

When a person contacts *the Good*, not only do they see a complete vision of reality, however brief, that reveals the fact of human and planetary unity, but they have now discovered within themselves the guiding light of the soul that can lead them safely and expediently from one stage to the next to express the divine Idea that fortifies Creation more perfectly. As parts of the whole, each of us carries within us the life and consciousness capable of adequately responding to *the Good*. Cultivating recognition of this fact is our highest priority and guarantees the possibility of a better world. Common good leaders, sacrificing personal gain and adjusting their well-developed personalities to serve the common good, embody the will-*to-Good*, thus creating compelling ideals and innovative approaches that make *the Good* real for all.

When considering laws — how they are formed and by whom — as adaptive expressions of a society's presently realizable highest ideals based on *the Good* suggests an image of what can be that evokes a response from each of us to better ourselves and our circumstances. These laws, created through a political system, should cultivate possibilities in the lives of people bound by them that renew their spirit. Thus, the law becomes not only a framework of enforcement but likewise one of generative renewal for its people, culture, and civilization. This guideline is, of course, equally applicable to the rites, rituals, and practices that govern the fields of human living that give our lives meaning — education, religion, business, and social institutions.

Insisting that the law should not only be reactive, punishing bad actors, but proactive, articulating a vision for realizing our shared purpose, posits decision-making responsibility based on one's ability to recognize *the Good*, interpret its future possibilities, and intelligently adapt it to meet the present need and according to people's current capacity to comply. The ideal society may have neither abortions, capitalism, poverty, weapons, overuse of fossil fuels, etc. Policy and decision-makers must, however, demonstrate the requisite ability to formulate laws, structures, and practices that inspire our desire to conform to a binding present good and, simultaneously, strive to envision *the Good* for ourselves, eventually replacing compliance with shouldered responsibility.

One can argue that based on the present stage of human imperfection and in light of the goal to which humanity aims, such things as abortion and capitalism are imperfect expressions of a sensed divinity, as are all the ideas and ideals upon which our present culture and civilization are based. Freedom is their basis, providing equal opportunity for autonomy and responsibility when otherwise unobstructed by desires or ambitions run amok. These, too, shall pass.

Behind the clamor of anti-abortion, anti-capitalism, and anti-establishment or anti-elitism is a sensed forward step for humanity to regulate and transmute desire: to transform our world into one that valorizes spiritual aspirations rather than material possessions and comfort, accumulation of things, power, and that which only money can give: supremacy. An ordered, lovingly intelligent world is the underlying impetus despite some people's often antagonizing fervor. Nevertheless, as do many others, they recognize that the cause of many of our problems is overstimulation and unchecked desires. However, prioritizing *the Good* challenges us to reimagine and restructure systems and institutions over-reliant upon outcomes, externally imposed, to help people develop what is, for many, still an imperceptible capacity to will *the Good* for the Commons. Recognizing that *self-awareness*, *self-direction*, and *self-expression* are the preeminent qualities necessary for people to contribute rightly to the good of the whole, we build a new society that facilitates their proper development.

We resist undermining the will of individuals, groups, or nations vulnerable to the imposition of a stronger will because we understand that such interference hinders the full potential and flowering of the life within them. On the other hand, we restrain the strong-willed who might otherwise cause undue harm without violating their free choice. In the first instance, we recognize the need to nurture the proper development of the will. Meanwhile, for those whose will nature is already paramount, the goal must be to reorient it to seek the good of the whole as they learn to restrain themselves for the common good. This two-fold approach ensures that each person, group, and nation, oriented towards divine Purpose, becomes fully equipped to contribute the best of who they are for the betterment of the world. In this way, we provide the opportunity and conditioning that help us all discover *the Good* within us and use it to serve the common good. When we learn to handle correctly and eventually elevate desire into constructive, creative activity and service benefiting humankind, sex and money will find their proper place in our lives. *Is it possible for us to imagine a future where having mastered ourselves, we handle sex, money, and power to further divine purpose alone?*

Lurking behind every ideal is a divine *Idea*, says Bradford that, while clothing itself in many forms, remains that *something outside, something beyond, ... humanity must have to strive for, to hope for.* And, once grasped, the Idea can be more readily attained. To arrive at these underlying principles requires common good leaders to seek the causes behind the effects. Doing so makes it possible to create new ideals and solutions to deal with what appear to be many diverse issues and all at once.

Transmuting desire into aspiration under soul guidance begins to control our excesses and bring personality and soul into alignment, eventually yielding the use of the personality to soul or group purpose. At a higher turn, the impassioned aspirations inspired — as they are — by contact with *the Good* to which many people stridently adhere are resolved through the tenets articulated by the Buddha: discrimination, dispassion, and detachment. Their persistent application awakens the intuition and imposes the light of pure reason upon our lower minds, revealing the concrete mind as inherently calculating, duplicitous, and separative, irrespective of how high our aspirations are. We come to recognize "the mind is the slayer of the Real."

Living as souls, we discover the Way that resolves all dualities and cleavages, revealing spirit and matter as one and the same. As many spiritual teachers have previously taught, spirit is matter at its highest, and matter (and its limitless permutations) is spirit at its lowest. Somewhere between the two, we locate ourselves, our ideals, and every human and nonhuman life expression. Wherever we find ourselves, our nation, and the world, we can be assured that we are in the process of *becoming* and manifesting upon earth step-by-step, civilization by civilization, and life after life, a higher aspect of divinity. As humanity evolves, we recognize our role in an ever greater whole, leading from self-consciousness to group consciousness and, eventually, universal consciousness. A new opportunity and leap forward presents itself to our humanity, encouraging us to leave behind the fallacy of separativeness and division and embrace the fact of the one humanity and one life that sustains all.

So long as our world exists, what will persist is the constant tension between the *Idea* and the ideal — freedom and restraint — divine Purpose and its materialization — the Will of God and the "little wills" of people who must strive to implement it. Our attempts to contact, rightly interpret, and manifest *the Good* help individuals and humanity as a whole resolve this tension as we become conscious creators below (on Earth) of what exists in the heavens above: *the Great Good*.

It is essential that we understand the will of God as a supreme energy or life force to which all of creation owes its existence and, in varying degrees, responds. The self-conscious human being, having free will, distinguishing itself from the lower kingdoms of nature — the vegetable, animal, and mineral — becomes equipped to do more than unthinkingly respond to this sweeping energy. Human minds are the gate-Way that bridges the Will and Purpose of God and the kingdoms lower than the human, making the one humanity a receiver and transmitter to the kingdoms below in the same way the Hierarchy or Kingdom of Souls is to the human kingdom from the higher spiritual kingdoms. The spiritual Hierarchy includes enlightened personalities or souls committed to loving the whole — to a greater or lesser extent — making them outposts of the will-*to-Good*, which is the will of God as it unfolds in time and space.

Evolution defines our planet's graduated approach to perfection, benevolently effectuated through an intelligent and loving understanding by those who love, serve, and guide the human race. All people have the innate capacity to participate consciously and to lend their support to the work of the Hierarchy of Souls. Yet the realization of this fact and skill-in-action for each of us differs tremendously. The door is, however, open to all who strive to love and serve the common good. Equally, it is closed to any who, through deliberate choice and not through ignorance (as many today still are), refuse the invitation of intelligent, loving service.

God doesn't give specific directives to individuals. His stupendous Reason or *the Great Good* permeates all. It is persistent and unchanging Thought, capable of adaptation for service to the good of the whole by souls focused upon the mental plane, sensitive to group needs, and dedicated to group progress. To them, *the Good* can be rightly intuited, interpreted, and individually and collectively shaped into ideals that serve people and the planet. Responsibility for these results lies with the individual or group creating them. Therefore, we must undertake our work humbly, understanding that we are prone to errors because of the imperfection of the present forms we embody. As a result, one might correctly discern that even the slightest direct contact of a single unit of life within the vastness of our planet with the directed energy or Thought of God would shatter the form immediately.

We can better understand the impacts of this energy if we relate it to the sense of falling in love that at least momentarily makes a person lose sight of the strict boundaries between themselves and the other. Entirely and all at once, those who fall in love become one with the object of their desire: a person, house, car, ideology, nation, religion, and so on. There is a shattering of the separative identity and fusion, however briefly, with that which is loved. People who have fallen in love often say that they can't bear to be apart from one another, would give their life for the other, follow the other's lead without question or hesitation, and sacrifice their all for someone, an ideal, or a cause. These are ways the not-self or the personality seeks to integrate and fuse with something it deems greater than itself. But in our infancy, the pure love energy that permeates our universe merges with the individual and group forces of desire, attaching to one form or another what is impersonal and intended to touch, nourish, and revitalize all life upon our planet, reaching ever nearer perfection.

Imagine, then, the impact of a nanosecond of concentrated Thought upon our tiny life by the Intelligence responsible for creating and directing the whole of our planetary life. Would it be possible to maintain a separative identity and form after contact with the One Self when many of us are still so willing (and desperate even) to lose ourselves in other not-selves with such ease? The desire then to merge with Love, Whose name is God and is the most profound energy within the universe, would be incomparable. Thankfully, such is not the case. For this reason, only the self-aware, self-directed, and self-expressing personality as it becomes increasingly detached and inclusive (and therefore an integrated and fused soul) can even begin to withstand contacts with higher spiritual energies as are all who have fit Themselves as Members of the Kingdom of God and are outposts of the Mind of God. Their thoughts (as energy) are directed to humanity, awakening, enlightening, and assisting our progress. Their Membership in the spiritual Hierarchy and subsequent nearness to the seat of the Father (God) is wholly determined by their conscious and willing subordination of personal will to the will of God. They have no other aim but to assist in working out divine Purpose, in unwavering coordination and cooperation with and for the common good, adapting, modifying, and implementing God's Purpose and (Loving) Plan on earth. Therefore, we can understand civilization at any point in time as the result of humanity's ability or lack thereof to channel and rightly direct the higher and differentiated energies and rhythms as they stream from God through the spiritual Hierarchy, reaching the minds of those who are becoming more mentally (rather than emotionally) focused and oriented towards *the Good*.

From God's perspective, forms, irrespective of their splendor, are a limitation. Regarded as an energy, God is transcendent and immanent and, therefore, equally alive with or without taking form. On a lesser scale, at the moment that an individual realizes that they are both human and divine — a personality and soul — they know that they, too, like the One in Whose body of manifestation they exist, persist: as souls, whether in form or formless, we *live*.

Detachment from forms or identifying with our lower self or others' personalities and instead relating to others as souls deepens identification with divinity and, simultaneously, permits us to help beautify the planetary form in which we live and move and have our being. Thus, the will of God, which is the will-*to-Good*, works out upon our planet through those who know themselves not only as personalities but equally as souls. By loving and serving the Plan, which is God's Purpose, adapted to world needs at any point in human history, our focus changes from the diversity of forms until we see only the souls of each and the unity of all.

Planetary equilibrium and universal cooperation are humanity's goals for the foreseeable future. To achieve these, we must strive to implement them in daily living for ourselves and through preserving and restoring right relations with others and all lives, seen and unseen.

As we become oriented to the soul, public opinion can conform to the new ideals taking shape in the minds and hearts of those impulsed by the common *Good*. Today, humanity is not what it once was. Stage-by-stage and sorry-by-sorry, we strive towards betterment, spiritual freedom, and revelation of the divine within us so that it may manifest through us. Wisdom, which must be the sought-after factor among leaders everywhere, recognizes the highest divinity for which a nation and humanity as a whole are presently capable of expressing.

When parents observe their child taking their first steps, gleefully teetering on tiptoes as they relish their newfound freedom of mobility, perhaps they share a furtive glance, acknowledging a shared vision for their child's future self. They see them pitching for the Los Angeles Dodgers. It was how the child ran towards them with their left arm outstretched, elbow bent just so that could only mean southpaw glory.[13]

For the parents, the vision is unmistakable, absolute. *But where to begin?* A regimented daily practice schedule at two would ensure failure and a likely call to child protective services. On the other hand, an active lifestyle that allows the child to enjoy the outdoors, playing, bouncing, frolicking in the grass, and, perhaps, attending live sporting events will nurture the vision without imposing it. As the years proceed and life happens, the parents' vision begins to sit alongside their child's vision for themselves. Their child, now a prodigious talent at fourteen, embraces their parent's vision full-throttle. Eventually, the parent's vision recedes because the child either fully embodies their vision or adopts an alternate one.

---

13   For a fascinating deep-dive into southpaws, see: Molyneux, Guy. "What Really Gives Left-Handed Pitchers Their Edge?" *FiveThirtyEight*, 17 Aug. 2020, fivethirtyeight.com/features/what-really-gives-left-handed-pitchers-their-edge/.

Similarly, America now sits on the threshold between the former paternalism that entrusts *the Good* to only a select few and a new cooperative autonomy that helps others glimpse this common purpose by creating conditions that make it possible for people to share in its benefits and obligations to an increasing degree. When the child's vision aligns with the parents — *unforced and adopted as their own* — the child will shoulder their responsibilities, make the sacrifices needed, and become an example that encourages others to seek the vision for themselves. On a larger scale, when leaders and decision-makers across all industries relied upon to establish the common good, graduate from the paternalistic practices of the past, and trust in the people's desire and ability to share and cooperate in the vision as conditions improve, they can help the nation demonstrate the reality — unbreakable and immovable — of *the Good*.

Selfless leaders willing to set aside personal gain to serve the common good, shed past paternalism, and instead embrace cooperative autonomy can help restore public trust and fuel the spread of goodwill. Americans are no longer content to be passive observers of their nation's trajectory; instead, they are fervently engaging in political action, unionizing, protesting, and creating community solutions to be active architects of change. This groundswell of awareness of others' suffering and response reflects a collective realization of a blossoming public will by which Americans insist their leaders no longer paternalistically coddle them. They are determined to take matters into their own hands, know and understand the issues, and actively contribute to creating a better nation. This vibrant and diverse movement demonstrates a growing willingness to embrace the responsibilities of democracy, emphasizing the importance of trust in the American people to rise to the occasion and shape a brighter future.

That the masses are often reactive and deluded by more powerful, malicious personalities is true. This present condition does not negate their desire for truth. Such personalities have, too often, co-opted or repressed the people's will to advance the selfish agendas of the few and, as a consequence, delayed humanity's spiritual progress and an improvement in material conditions. Only the countervailing accomplishments of the will-*to-Good* to resolve all problems and leave people more spiritually free can suffice. Economic, political, social, and institutional systems exist to serve the people. Common good leaders, motivated by the will-*to-Good*, indicating an inspired vision of what can be balanced with a compassionate understanding of what is and an unwavering commitment to serve can revive the nation's soul and unleash *the Good*. These are the leaders the people everywhere are searching for to respond with compassion, understanding, and wise action, trusting that they will lead for the common good, set aside personal gain, and, in doing so, inspire each of us to cultivate and give our best to the nation and world.

For the maturing human being becoming increasingly self-conscious and group conscious, this sensed duality creates tension and conflict. We are both self-aware of how the tumultuousness of today's world affects the quality of our lives and its more significant impact on society as a whole. Unlike the unknowing or the self-absorbed, common good leaders meet with circumstances throughout every aspect of their lives — personal, professional, and social — requiring a choice to either cling steadfastly to those things that shore up our egos or, instead, sacrifice our pride, ambition, proven skill-in-action, centrality, and the many proofs of our uniqueness and deservedness of high regard. When we commit to serve humanity, we can no longer delude ourselves. We see clearly the deception underlying our seemingly altruistic motives. We become painfully aware of how often our doing good for others masks our desire for acceptance and validation. Peering down at the soapboxes we've stood on, we face up to the fact that our publicly shared quips and takedowns were never intended to enlighten but to discredit and erase. We learn that the sword of truth is not something to wield against others but is that upon which we must immolate ourselves to free the soul from the prison of the separated self. The soul within every person, organization, and nation must free itself like the butterfly emerging from its cocoon, having been sufficiently nurtured and prepared within its protective casing for its next stage of life. But free itself it must. For us, the personality is the chrysalis developed over many lifetimes under soul guidance, not as an end unto itself but to eventually manifest the *life* waiting to emerge upon the material plane in all its perfected glory.

How readily do we make the necessary relinquishments to free the spirit within? Knowing that we have the power to get our way, how often do we recognize the greater good possible if we choose to stand down? To what degree do our organizational policies and practices further entrench competition, reward selfishness, and elevate its goals over the good of the whole? Daily living among family, friends, colleagues, and strangers allows us to recognize the many expressions of this conflict between rugged and cooperative individualism, personality and soul, and the individual and the Commons. The leaders of the human race know that they are powerful but also know that, as they are yet imperfect divine expressions of God, they must learn to temper that power with love. Others may love but fail to use the soul's power that is rightfully at their disposal (because they love!), having witnessed the grave misuses of power among those who do not yet love rightly. Together, these leaders must learn to wield the will-*to-Good* to transform humanity's lowest expressions of desire, aspiration, and will into Goodwill for all. They must strive to become self-aware, self-directing, and self-expressing agents for the group conscious soul to work upon them and, through them, to serve the common good.

Common good leaders are working to build a new civilization and culture that serves the greatest good for the greatest number amid the destruction currently underway of social and political institutions, economic paradigms, environmental conditions, and ideologies. They will not get everything right. Yet they will speak in terms of the whole and present practical and inclusive ideas, innovations, and solutions to create right relations among and between people and the planet. Common good leaders demonstrate the following characteristics:

1. They love humanity.
2. They recognize a *subjective unity*, linking them with one another and the people of goodwill everywhere based upon a shared understanding of humanity's next steps.
3. Their *diverse yet coordinated activities* arise from an inner realization of humanity's shared goal interpreted and worked out in all fields and levels of human endeavor to reach everyone in service to the common good.
4. They don't criticize others' efforts, leaving them free to serve as they see fit.
5. They are working in every field of human enterprise — *education, psychology, business, religion, finance and economics, politics and government, science, and artistic expression* — to build a new and better world for all.

Striving to recognize common good leaders and support their efforts through cultivating right relations and spreading goodwill in our homes, workplaces, places of worship, social groups, and wherever we find ourselves can help accelerate rebuilding and reconstruction on a local, national, and global scale. In recent centuries, America has exported strident individualism alongside frenzied extractive capitalist consumerism, depleting world resources and human flourishing. It has also spread technological innovations, democratic ideals, and education for the masses abroad and sounded a reverberating note of freedom. Like the individual, America must awaken and radiate its soul, using its purified and matured personality to improve life at home and abroad.

Returning to the life and example set forth for us by Christ, Whose demonstrated freedom from wrong thought, a controlling desire and wish life, and purposeless living revealed what is possible when the infinite divine will is given full expression through the finite personality of a human being of pure heart and an illuminated mind, provides correct orientation and guidance. Common good leaders, through experiment and experience, learn the true meaning of freedom. Through commitment to the divine Plan and service to humanity, we learn that only when a person stands unmoved by personal desires or outer circumstances and becomes an intelligent, self-willed outpost for divine will are we truly free.

Loving as Christ loved instantiates an outpouring of love from people to God and to one another and, as a result, permits world servers to guide the human race to *the Good* by its proliferation, radiating and magnetizing others through positive reinforcement instead of restrictive assertions ("Dos/Don'ts") and punitive consequences. Common good leaders, animated by the vision of *the Good*, equip themselves for greater service by rejecting the allure of material things, desire, and ambition. Then and only then can we who love and serve stand free. Through these devoted servers, the will-*to-Good* can flow, attracting others to *the Good* and an assumption of responsibility and participation in good works that make restrictive covenants unnecessary because people find it increasingly impossible to act contrary to *the Good*.

9.

CONVENING AND COOPERATING

THERE IS A tendency to insist that others, even those with whom we share an agreed outcome — ending homelessness and racism, making education less costly and more accessible, creating thriving cities and rural areas — see the problem precisely as we see it and adopt the causation we've ascribed, dictating a specific approach and solution, and then and only then can we find a way to work together. Aware that most of us lack the present capacity to think from the universal to the particular, we can increase cooperation by acknowledging this limited ability to see the whole, confirming our need to cooperate as a natural condition that we cannot bypass at this stage of human development. Thus, the need to collaborate is an innate evolutionary demand that enlarges and magnifies, simultaneously providing depth and breadth to confront challenges and develop multifaceted and multilevel changes that can reach everyone impacted. Simple solutions to complex problems don't mean uniformity of approach but rather a unity of purpose, inclusive of the needs of all stakeholders and responsive to the diverse perspectives needed to achieve results.

Humanitarians and all the people of goodwill worldwide recognize this period of polycrisis as the culmination of humanity's joint errors, which are too intricate to untangle and too numerous to apportion blame. From every nation and every class, the people of goodwill recognize a mutual desire to move forward to better days. They also know the necessity of forgiveness, removing the stigma of transgressions so that the whole of humanity can unite in the shared purpose of *unleashing the Good* among all people everywhere. We must also recognize that moving forward unitedly requires acknowledging how fixed ideas can hinder our willingness to work cooperatively to address societal issues and foster a shared vision for the future. When individuals become entrenched in their beliefs, they may resist compromise, dialogue, or collaboration with those with different views. This impractical idealism can hinder exploring new, innovative solutions to complex problems.

To foster a future focused on the common good, the people of goodwill must be open-minded and open-hearted. Doing so can help us move forward unburdened by our collective past mistakes and, instead, focused and directed to freely and imaginatively create a new future. Embracing flexibility in thinking can pave the way for collaboration and the development of creative approaches that benefit society as a whole. Forgiveness allows us to move forward together without feeling as if we must advocate for the rights of one group or those of another, refusing to settle for less than the good of the whole.

When encountering hate and discrimination, we must address them decisively to end the harm, offering the opportunity for redemption to the person or group causing the harm. We learn to correct and repair cleavages that restore wholeness rather than embarrass, shame, or cast off. This idea is the impetus behind many restorative practices, which, when rightly instituted, can provide a lifeline as my uncle demonstrated with each *"Good morning,"* met with taut reluctance, giving *The Rifleman*, again and again, an opportunity to rediscover his humanity and reveal his divinity.

Many tools to aid us in having challenging conversations exist. If you're using one that recognizes the voices of diverse stakeholders and keeps people at the table, you're already well on your way. The Right Relations Protocol is a tool created to help us collaborate with others with whom we recognize a shared goal. Through its three practices, it can help people and organizations working for the common good develop a new habit that eventually expresses their soul nature in due time. These are:

- **Recognize the many paths to truth.** Recognize that each person is on a pathway that leads to the realization that we are each a part of a greater whole. Some are nearer to this realization than others. But the destination is guaranteed. Practice recognizing the divine or spiritual aspect within each, unifying each to all that is.

In challenging moments, we can ask: How can I help others acknowledge and express their higher, spiritual nature (and, in so doing, nurture my own divine expression)?

- **Practice (loving) detachment.** Realize how our thoughts, words, and actions reinforce separation rather than the goal of unity. Practice recognizing when we are thinking, speaking, and acting in ways that deepen our sense of separateness from others. Loving detachment and indifference help turn our attention away from the diversity of forms, enabling us to identify the essence that unites each to all.

When encountering new people, new ideas, and different ways of being that clash with our own, we can ask: How are my thoughts, words, and actions reinforcing my or others' sense of separation rather than unity?

- **Assess intent.** Ask whether we and others are motivated by a more selfless or selfish intent, increasing our capacity to create workable solutions beneficial to all. Practice recognizing when we are living more as our group-conscious spiritual selves or self-conscious personalities.

When we are in the self-protective mode, which naturally arises in times of fear or duress, we can ask: What motivates me to take action right now? To what extent do I fully understand the circumstances and needs of others involved to ensure that my response furthers the common good rather than only my own?

When these three practices are implemented consistently with time set aside for honest reflection regarding our success or failure, we will find that we develop our capacity to recognize the divine in others, identify when our thoughts, words, and actions reinforce our own or others' sense of separateness, and make the needed adjustments that will encourage us and others to live more as group conscious souls rather than self-conscious personalities. Achieving these will enable us to be instrumental in building the bridges that permit us and others to create solutions to our world problems, offering us a way forward (and here's the key!) that is self-initiated and mutually affirms each person's part in a greater whole. Complete understanding and genuine, selfless service expand when we consciously identify with all human and planetary life.

It's helpful to consider the essential choice presented to us in everyday interactions with family, coworkers, and strangers between evoking their personality (separating, dividing, self-centered) or soul (unifying, group-oriented, inclusive) aspect. Our goal is to begin to relate to and engage people as souls and to enlarge humanity's capacity to connect soul-to-soul or soul-to-personality rather than as differentiated and largely egoistic personalities. An intention to engage as a soul and, therefore, to awaken the soul (or inclusive aspect) of others is of paramount importance. It is not easy to maintain a soul disposition at first, necessitating poised self-reflection to ensure that we're not relating to people in a way that intentionally or unintentionally reinforces their exclusionary or (this not that) personality.

We must pay attention to how we consciously or unconsciously inflame the separative personality for ourselves or others, recognizing its identity hinges on prioritizing its likes and dislikes and qualities that set it apart and, too often, above others. Individuals, organizations, and nations, relating as personalities, unwittingly reinforce separateness and bring out (as far as the advancing humanity is concerned) the worst in others by bolstering either their own or others' selfish (personality) rather than selfless (soul) tendencies.

Of course, we can observe this in many daily, conspicuous and subtle interactions. Two examples may help elucidate our daily plight to cultivate right relations among all we encounter:

When students first discovered that I maintained a vegan diet, some taunted me with whatever meat was being served on campus that day. Others teased me and, at the same time, counted on me to buy the fruits and vegetables they grew as participants in our school's agriculture program. For some students, my diet offended their way of being through no fault of mine. If I allowed it, their taunts and teasing could have pushed me to respond in ways that reinforced veganism as my choice and, in doing so, negated their own. That's not what happened, of course.

At every opportunity, I reminded students that they could eat and love meat as much as they chose. I explained to them that I had grown up eating meat, why I stopped, how my choice was what was best for me, and that they were equally free to decide what was best for them. In due time, some students became curious enough to ask questions and try vegan foods. A devoted meat eater finally said during another day of ridiculing my meal that I was "the good kind of vegan" because I "wasn't judgy like a lot of people and didn't try to force it on anyone." Refusing to assert my identity as a vegan, which in my case distinguished me from most of my students, allowed them to create space in their lives to include at least the "the good kind of vegan," which was more than would have been possible if I took a principled stand on being a vegan and reminded them of it as often as possible. In other words, I remained principled in my choices even as I related to them as emerging souls on their own journey to discover the *truth* they most needed to move onward and upward, and they responded with openness and expansion.

Another example I'd like to share is a seemingly inconsequential conversation about the weather that quickly erupted, catching me off guard. I realized how easily it is to ignite personality reactions if one is not careful. I should begin by saying moving back to the South as the planet heats up is, for me, a tough pill to swallow. How my body is made (e.g., don't blame me, but the one who made me!) doesn't permit proper acclimation to extreme temperatures. The body likes what the body likes, which is a temperate climate hovering between 32 - 70 degrees Fahrenheit. But if I had to choose, I'd accept below-freezing temperatures to extreme heat any day. Thus, my dilemma. Understanding this about myself, I don't typically discuss summer temperatures among the people who like it hot. Again, these are just personal preferences like eating or not eating meat. And even if and when our preferences, taken together, have a deleterious impact on the environment as some believe meat eating does, we must seek a resolution from the level where one becomes capable of considering the concerns of the whole: the soul.

On a mild December day with temperatures in the mid-50s, someone casually suggested I must be hot since I wore a t-shirt. I made the mistake of saying yes, which provoked a mini-tirade. As the person renounced colder temperatures in favor of the upper 80s and 90s, their ire seemed to suggest that "me and my kind," whose imperfect bodies suffer in the heat, were to blame for a typical winter day in Nashville. Caught off guard, I had to take pointed steps to engage my higher Self to extricate me from this dynamic safely and gracefully. I don't remember what I said, but whatever it was, it worked. More importantly, it provided a profound lesson about the sly ways we fall back into relating as personalities rather innocently if we're not careful.

Of course, we're allowed to like and not like whatever we choose. Yet we can find ourselves in unnecessary confrontations by emphasizing our differences, however minute and nonessential they seem. Interacting as souls with other souls or personalities minimizes division. It offers opportunities to include others and find commonalities (or at least not be distracted by differences) because only the influence of the higher Self (soul) can tame the roar of the personality. In this way, we lift others higher by straining ourselves not to make them better but by refusing to assert ourselves in profound and subtle ways that provoke the lower tendency in all of us that seeks to reinforce our differences. Our reward is to realize that by blending within ourselves the lower and higher aspects and striving to live as souls, we start to bring out the best in people despite their usual selfish and self-centered ways and our own. And just to be clear, I am okay with the weather, *weathering*. Of course, humanity must strive to create and sustain a balanced biosphere for us and the nonhuman lives for which we are responsible. In the meantime, if you speak to me about the weather, my only response will be: all good.

The time for convening and cooperating is not the time for self-assertion. Whenever we emphasize what separates us, including preferences, identity, affiliations, etc., we risk failing to recognize our shared purpose. Differences close our eyes to the universal. However, prioritizing the universal or the common good doesn't diminish the specific or the validity of the individual; instead, it reorders the focus from the universal to the part. In this way, people seeking new ideas and ways of working together to address the political, social, and economic challenges created by the more self-centered, rugged individualists (as are all national and world problems) first determine an outcome good for the whole that can then be adapted to the needs of the various groups and individuals impacted.

Reorienting our focus to think from the universal to the specific rather than from the part to the whole is the objective of Common Good Education, an online course I've created for teachers, parents, psychologists, social workers, and others dedicated to helping youth develop their highest potential in service to the whole. As we strengthen this reorientation, we learn to prioritize the common good over personal gain and, at the same time, develop our individual capacities to serve the needs of the whole. Eventually, we recognize individuality and universality as one and the same.

We are Divinity manifesting in diversity and, therefore, sons of God seeking to express His sublime nature, which is *Love*, more fully. We increasingly realize that our identification with the whole is what reveals our true *Identity*. And remaining separate from the whole, we recognize that we can never know or express the fullness of our being. Only when people, organizations, groups, and nations willingly sacrifice self-serving pursuits in service to the greater *Good* do we become whole.

We are part of something bigger than ourselves, and that something (a family, nation, world, and universe) requires something from each that only they can give. Becoming group conscious, we know within ourselves that we are the whole and an imperishable part of that whole. We learn to think from the universal to the specific, retaining our individuality and, at the same time, becoming something greater than ourselves. We seek to become whole by serving the whole.

Eventually, in consciousness and cooperative activity, we set aside the individual (and self-serving) personality and, instead, know ourselves to be an Impersonal individuality and equally the One Humanity, dedicated to contributing the best of who we are and are becoming to further group progress.

We can expect many missteps on the road to consecrating right relations. Yet, as we strive to recognize others' divine nature, reorient our focus from the material to the spiritual, and master our thoughts, words, and actions through the increasingly selfless sacrifice of our personal desires, aspirations, and will to work alongside others to realize a common good, we build bridges linking each of us to every person, every nation, and the entire life of our planet. These self-initiated and mutually affirming bridges result in our collective highest good.

10.

THE SOUL OF AMERICA

DURING VARIOUS TIMES in our nation's history, leaders have called upon citizens to recognize the soul of the nation. Reflecting on these moments tells us that during times of great internal strife (attempt to avoid the Civil War) or external threat (9/11 Terrorist attacks), presidents Abraham Lincoln and George W. Bush sought to remind us of the shared purpose and the sacred covenant codified in the U.S. Constitution that reads:

We the People of the United States, in Order to form a more perfect Union, establish Justice, insure domestic Tranquility, provide for the common defense, promote the general Welfare, and secure the Blessings of Liberty to ourselves and our Posterity, do ordain and establish this Constitution for the United States of America.

A plea for the common good reminds us of our shared goal and further delineates the steps required today to bring us nearer the ideal. Individuals, organizations, and nations are all in the process of *becoming*. We are living organisms on a living planet that is in constant flux. The aphorism, "Change is the only constant in life," (Heraclitus) liberates us to grapple — intelligently and optimistically — with who we are while holding steadfastly to the vision of who we can be. A more perfect union is our destiny. Yet, we can only realize perfection when the soul of America shines forth, joining with the souls of other nations to create a more outstanding beauty upon this planet than humanity has ever witnessed.

Historian and author John Meacham reminds us in *The Soul of America: The Battle for Our Better Angels* that "The war between the ideal and the real, between what's right and what's convenient, between the larger good and personal interest is the contest that unfolds in the soul of every American." This raging duality is the process of *becoming*. Taking our development in hand, we begin each lifetime with an opportunity to grow wiser, not just get older. A nation's life and rebirths provide a similar opportunity over a longer period for it, too, to reveal its hidden majesty: its soul.

Do we just get older, or do we mature?

There is an undeniable defiance in insisting that the Soul of America *IS*. Despite appearances to the contrary, the vision accorded by America's soul beckons each of us — *tired, poor, huddled masses yearning to breathe free* — with the sound of freedom. But not any freedom, instead a more profound and spiritual freedom, providing not only bread for the body but food for the soul. Economic relief and the spread of goodwill are the shared responsibility of leaders and the people. We need cross-sector collaborations that acknowledge our problems, set aside personal gain in favor of the common good, and lay the groundwork to build a brighter future for America.

When considering Christ's example, we often discuss His teachings, miracles, death, and resurrection. Yet, His most profound impact was His radiance, magnetically attracting and strengthening humankind's dim lights and little wills. "Light of the World," "Bread of Life," and "Resurrection and the Life" are descriptors ascribed to our Elder Brother. He was a living soul and, therefore, capable of pouring light into a dark world, feeding the masses, and resurrecting the spirit of humanity entombed by materialism. He surrounded Himself with imperfect men because the salvaging of humanity was not only His but theirs to do. Doing our part has always been part of the plan. This same World Teacher, called by different names — Lord Maitreya, the Imam Mahdi, and the Messiah — exists among many of the world's religions. One need not be a Christian to recognize His life as inaugurating and providing the pattern by which every person, every nation, and humanity as a whole might create "life more abundantly" when inspired by and dedicated to the common good.

The historical Christ, a God and man, stood as an intermediary between humanity and God. He is Love-Wisdom, uniting the will of God and Its intelligent expression through (hu)Man (i.e., the one who *thinks*). From the human perspective, love invoking God's will is essentially the will-*to-Good*, wisely adapting and translating *the Good* for immediate use by humanity, thus evoking new and motivating ideals that further human and planetary evolution. Buddha's Noble Eightfold Path, teaching the middle Way that leads to enlightenment, was the precursor to Christ's revealed perfection. Following Buddha's Teachings, we seek a changeless state, no longer pulled this way or that. Instead, we discover the Way, that narrow path leading between the dueling opposites that tear us asunder: pleasure and pain, having and not-having, success and failure, belonging and rejection, self-assertion and self-denial, among many others.

Through detachment, discrimination, and dispassion, we purify the self-seeking, lower self through contact with the group-conscious, higher Self. Through blending and fusing these competing aspects of ourselves, we inevitably discover the middle Way or what the Buddha called nonduality, wherein all opposites meet and merge. What we once perceived as vast differences, reality reveals as variation masking an underlying unity. By uniting personality and soul within ourselves, we project a unifying perspective onto opposing and seemingly unresolvable personal, group, and world challenges. Through persistence, refusing a blissful idealism or an arid realism, we discover that we are wise conduits for restoring equilibrium and harmony in our homes, workplaces, communities, and nations. This ability to unite what at one time appeared decidedly different brings suffering to an end for the enlightened human being, organization, nation, and humanity as a whole. Cooperative individualism replaces the once rugged, selfish individualism that further divides, separates, and, as a result, disguises the Real, the Beautiful, and the True, which is the indissoluble unity of all human and planetary life. The illuminated (cooperative) personality is no longer deluded by the appearance of variety, seeing only the one life appearing in different forms, permitting all who attain enlightenment, as the Buddha instructed, to become a pure channel through which the will-*to-Good* can flow.

The Christ went further in His expression. Whereas the Buddha taught us how to fit ourselves to become conscious transmitters of the will of God (the will-*to-Good*), Christ demonstrated the perfected outcome of our efforts to blend soul and personality. The fused soul-personality of a person, group, organization, or nation performs a dual function that permits all who come to embody it, as did the Christ, interpretative facility, and creative application of *the Good*. Humanity must recognize the result of its evolutionary goal as becoming sensitive to the two poles of its being: Life and its intelligent (creative) expression.

Humanity's proper role, resulting from conscious spiritual development, is bridging the divide between divinity and its unfolding visible perfection. Through trained minds and compassionate hearts focused on *the Good*, common good leaders evoke the will-*to-Good* by developing and circulating inspired spiritual ideals and practical solutions cultivated through contact with *the Good,* stimulating right relations and goodwill among all people. Christ made this opportunity possible by opening the gateway that will eventually allow God's will to manifest perfectly on earth under the leadership and guidance of the enlightened who know themselves as souls. These spiritual-minded and humanitarian world servers belong to the Kingdom of Souls, identified not by proclamation of their holiness or divine rights but by their sacrifice and selfless service for the common good.

These Members of a new spiritual Kingdom are exponents of Christ not because they delineate themselves as Christians but because they love wisely, strive to meet the needs of all who suffer, carry within them the vision irrespective of the surrounding appearances of human failings, and know *the Good* because they persist in radiating *the Good* through their thoughts, words, and deeds even, at times, at significant cost to themselves. They are the bridge linking Heaven and Earth, ensuring continuity of the vision and radiance of *the Good* to lead humanity ever forward into life more abundant. Through Christ and discovering the Christ within, humanity can know true freedom from all suffering and life everlasting.

Christ, the World Teacher, remains with us and in us, guiding us to recognition and full participation in the Kingdom of God. Its members help Christ to fulfill His promise, resurrecting matter into Heaven so that eventually, the objective world more truly reflects the divine. Matter becomes spiritualized, remaking this earthly (hell) into a spiritual Heaven. Soul and personality blend and fuse. Members of this spiritual Kingdom awakened to the Christ within prepare the Way. *The Good* opens the Way into the Kingdom of Souls. There is no more excellent vision than Christ, the perfected son of God, to which present humanity can attain and no greater instruction than that left to us by the Buddha to deliver us from all evil.

Battling for the Soul of America isn't a call to arms but a call to love, impulsed by will. It is the will-*to-Good*, combining recognition of our shared responsibility for existing problems and a cooperative intent to solve them for the common good. The solutions must be practical and tangible. They must replace fear with hope in the lives of the masses. They must kindle the willingness of each of us to develop our highest potential so that we, too, can serve because we know ourselves to be an intrinsic part of this nation and the one humanity.

11.

A CITY UPON A HILL

IN A TIME when the nation and world face pressing challenges, the need for common good leadership has never been more evident. By cultivating leaders whose dedication to the public good supersedes self-aggrandizement, we can inspire a global movement toward unity, trust, and positive change. Through collaborative efforts and a commitment to shared progress, we can pave the way for a future where humanity's betterment is as dear to each of us as our own success.

Setting aside personal gain to benefit the common good releases individuals, groups, and nations from the damage that rugged individualism has reaped upon humanity and the planet. The need for self-initiated, voluntary sacrifice of selfish interests to the shared vision, slowly coming into view due to the preponderance of worldwide pain, now confronts us. The humanitarians and people of goodwill in every nation are rallying to respond. In the U.S., these servers are perpetually aware of the growing crises — rising economic inequality, political fragmentation, social unrest, environmental degradation, mental health issues, lack of institutional faith, social mistrust, etc. — and, increasingly, leavened by the realization of the need for multi-sector collaborative "all hands on deck" approaches to resurrect the spirit of humanity and our nation from this self-made tomb of death and decay.

Working with focused, directed intent alongside others who share a love for humanity, recognize the infallible interconnectedness of all people, nations, and life upon our planet, and willingly set aside personal ambitions and aspirations for the benefit of the whole can and will bring relief and release to lead our nation from darkness to light, from chaos to order, from the cult of personality to the cult of goodwill, from tyranny to freedom, and from imperfection to a nearer realization of *the Good*.

Common good leaders work for spiritual uplift, not merely to alleviate material suffering. They improve present conditions because they know that doing so is the most suitable way to validate *the Good* and reveal the good within us. The soul within is the quiet voice that, in due time, must rise above the clamor of life's many distractions. Such leaders seek to create the conditions for people, organizations, and nations to access *the Good* within, to lend their efforts to manifest the Plan for world betterment and peace, and usher in right relations between people and the planet. Today, many thousands worldwide work for the common good, and many millions await opportunity. We can unleash *the Good* and realize a more perfect world for the benefit of all by finding each other, mutually supporting each other's efforts, and leaving others free to undertake responsibility and work out the Plan as they strive to recognize what is theirs to do.

A materialist orientation recognizes humankind as divided into the classes producing material life — oppressor-oppressed, feudal lords-peasants, slave owner-slave, and capitalist-worker. Yet, our history is replete with rebellions and revolutions arising from an innate desire not only for better material conditions but to express our divine nature more fully. That the results of humanity's spiritual demand to express its creativity, beauty, and intelligence have been, too often, reduced to improved material conditions, however slight and short-lived, is true. Yet the impetus driving us to seek an ever higher expression of what we are remains equally true.

Before the Great Depression, a crisis point in U.S. history, paving the way for America's New Deal and creating the largest middle class in world history, wealth was highly concentrated among a small portion of the population. The robber barons of the Gilded Age — Andrew Carnegie, Cornelius Vanderbilt, John D. Rockefeller, JP Morgan, and others — were so-called captains of industry whose selfish and often ruthless business practices helped them amass large fortunes. These and other wealthy individualists and corporations enjoyed unprecedented prosperity, while most Americans struggled with stagnant wages and limited economic opportunities. Sound familiar? The stock market crash of 1929 triggered a panic and a severe financial crisis, including bank failures, reduced consumer spending, and widespread unemployment, precipitating the Great Depression, which persisted through much of the 1930s. The New Deal was President Franklin D. Roosevelt's response, initiating a series of ambitious government programs to stimulate economic recovery and social reform, providing the foundation for a robust middle class.

A gradual chipping away at material gains over previous decades, beginning in the 1970s, concomitantly eroded the middle class. A combination of policies and practices — tax cuts for high-income earners and corporations, outsourcing of jobs to countries with cheaper labor and fewer regulations, deregulation allowing for greater consolidation and monopoly among certain sectors, declining union membership and weakening of labor protections, erosion of social safety nets, rising education, healthcare, and housing costs, stagnant wages, and financialization, producing more paper money as opposed to productive economic activity — served to restore and increase previous levels of material inequality. A short-lived and relative peace is the guaranteed outcome when we relegate the hunger for more to seeking and acquiring merely material rather than spiritual wealth. America and humanity as a whole are at a crossroads, again presented with a new opportunity to better conditions based on either dividing ourselves materially according to class and other impermanent and so-called identities, repeating a cycle of what will inevitably be an even shorter-lived material peace for some smaller few. Or, assimilating into a formidable group of cooperative individualists whose stand is not against the still self-seeking rugged individualists but on behalf of all people, nations, and the planet to provide those conditions — social, economic, environmental, political — that inspire and provide each with the requisite means to develop the best within themselves in service to the whole.

A new distinction between selfish and selfless individuals, groups, companies, and nations lays the foundation for creating a new culture based on the common good. Among all nations, all classes, all races, all genders, and all political groups are people whose ideas and actions indicate their desire to work cooperatively to achieve the greatest good for the greatest number. Such individuals have all the capacities of the rugged individualists, the former feudal lords, the gilded gentry, the robber barons, and the so-called elite or ruling class, but through their own volition have substituted selflessness for selfishness and group good for personal and political gain. These servers of humanity are the group to which all humanitarians and spiritual people must align themselves to make *the Good* a reality for all.

Learning to prioritize the common good over personal gain transforms society from one primarily created and sustained by selfish personalities to one transfigured and beautified by souls. Cooperative individualists, increasingly aware of human and planetary needs and motivated to help address these issues, set about to better themselves to become more useful in service. The choice each of us must make is whether we encase ourselves more deeply in a selfish individualism with its dire consequences for all life on our planet or adopt a conscious intention to embrace a more selfless individualism to achieve a new nation and new world better fit for the more intelligent, loving, and understanding humanity we are becoming.

"A Model of Christian Charity" is a famous sermon delivered by John Winthrop in 1630 to the Massachusetts Bay Colony Puritan settlers. According to historian Perry Miller, Winthrop's sermon, emphasizing the idea of a "city upon a hill," suggesting that the Puritans' community should serve as a model of Christian charity and virtue for others to follow best affirms America's origins and its purpose. Regarding society "not as an aggregation of individuals, but as an organism functioning for a definite purpose, with all parts subordinate to the whole, all members contributing a definite share," Miller sought to articulate and remind Americans of our shared purpose based upon the common good. Reflecting on Miller's influence to enunciate America's origins, Abram C. Van Engen, in *City on a Hill: A History of American Exceptionalism*,[14] says that Miller believed that Winthrop's sermon was "the first articulate statement

---

14   Van Engen, Abram C. *City on a Hill - a History of American Exceptionalism.* Yale University Press, 2020.

of community, a sermon expounding the idea that America would be dedicated to the life of the mind." In other words, according to Van Engen, Miller "read in Winthrop's text a monumental testimony against the basic premises of the American Dream." Miller, perhaps, failed to foresee "a city upon a hill" appropriated to celebrate individual freedom, material prosperity, and American power (Van Engen, p. 255). Reclaiming America's origins and purpose recognizes the existence of an immutable common goal whose demonstration is continually in flux as it emerges again and again from the ashes of its own destruction. If a "city upon a hill" captures an idea of American exceptionalism, indicating a belief in a unique role in the world, it must return to its origins as Winthrop crafted in the imagination of the Puritans, calling forth remembrance of our raison d'être,

> ...*to do justly, to love mercy, to walk humbly with our God. For this end, we must be knit together in this work as one man, we must entertain each other in brotherly affection, we must be willing to abridge ourselves of our superfluities, for the supply of others' necessities, we must uphold a familiar commerce together in all meekness, gentleness, patience and liberality; we must delight in each other, make others' conditions our own, rejoice together, mourn together, labor and suffer together, always having before our eyes our commission and community in the work, our community as members of the same body. So shall we keep the unity of the spirit in the bond of peace.*[15]

---

15   John Winthrop: "A Modell of Christian Charity." *Sage American History* http://sageamericanhistory.net/colonial/docs/winthrop.htm. Access September 21, 2023.

It is true that the U.S., like Great Britain, Russia, France, and other nations, has a distinct and vital role to play in furthering human progress. It is equally true that nations are, themselves, personalities in some stage or another between demonstrating selfishness or greater selflessness. Like the individual, a nation's exceptionalism can only come into view when they know themselves to be part of a greater whole and seek to develop their capacities to serve the whole. Each nation becomes, then, a "city upon a hill," shouldering its rightful share of responsibility in world service. Doing so, they realize they are no more or less exceptional than all other peoples and nations.

At this time, the will-*to-Good* must distinguish America and its people. We are a nation of ambitious strivers and spiritual seekers, wealth hoarders and philanthropic givers, humanitarians and self-seekers, close-fisted and open-hearted. We are, as yet, a nation in the process of *becoming*. We are becoming a new nation because we are oriented to the common good. Unleashing *the Good* can be our contribution to humankind, demonstrably improving world conditions with great speed and effectiveness if we begin today. All capable people must understand emerging ideas, interpret them for the common good, recognize others working along similar lines, and maintain a selflessness that always seeks the greatest good for the greatest number. The result will be a recognition and blossoming of the soul of America on full display, a bright light in the world, drawing to itself others seeking to share in its destiny: its freedom as well as its duty.

The common good can be the basis for a new American Dream, restoring its original intent to further the interests of all rather than the few, to pierce the veils of our collective imaginings that have accumulated and grown stronger amidst self-willed ambitions and aspirations. Learning to prioritize the common good over personal gain can become a new way of life through which we steadily let go of the things that no longer serve the new vision as we begin to grasp and embody it as our own. By becoming receptive to *the Good*, we recognize new possibilities to improve our nation and world. As our commitment to manifesting the Plan for the common good grows, so does our ability to relinquish our personal will to serve the good of the whole. No longer isolated and imprisoned by our selfish personalities, we discover each other anew and work cohesively to do our part to unleash *the Good*.

Let us become that city upon a hill, radiating the inherent good that resides within each of us: *the Good* rooted in what is true, beautiful, and ultimately best for the common good. Let us be a nation untrammeled by our past transgressions so that all people and nations might see in us the hope and glory of rebirth possible for the entire world. Let us embody universalism, love for humanity, and self-restraint as markers of our true identity as souls. Let us rise above our differences, embrace our shared humanity, and work together unified in purpose to create a brighter and more harmonious future for all. Let us strive to serve wherever we find ourselves to expand our capacity to be of greater service. Let us cultivate right relations between all people, all nations, and all life. Let us trust in *the Good*, work for *the Good*, live for *the Good*, and will *the Good* for the common good.

EPILOGUE

THE GREAT INVOCATION

TO BRING ABOUT world betterment at this most challenging time in human history tasks common good leaders with overcoming their prejudices, pride, ambition, feelings of futility, and aspirational fixations to recognize similarities of objectives, ideals, and methods, permitting effective collaboration where possible and ensuring harmlessness to all. Such dedicated world servers exist in every nation, government, political party, religion, race, ethnicity, and class. Their massed intent has yet to be fully mobilized for the helping of humanity. Group consciousness must unite us to renewed spiritual efforts to bring about the restoration demanded by the masses everywhere.

People around the world, when rightly taught, learn to distinguish and bridge the gap between the self-oriented personality and its higher counterpart, the group-oriented soul. Still, higher development exists, but for most human beings, the immediate possibility is becoming a soul-infused personality: an individual self-aware and oriented to the common *Good*.

The Great Invocation is a world prayer first released by Djwahl Kuhl, a Tibetan teacher and Master of the Wisdom, in 1945 to aid humanity's recognition of the spiritual Hierarchy of our planet and those perfected "sons of God who are also sons of men" who, throughout many ages and civilizations, have inspired, illuminated, and led humanity onward. It has been translated into almost seventy languages and dialects and used by millions. In practice, it is a universal spiritual project that includes people of all faiths and those motivated by humanitarian ideals. It is an act of service to humanity.

Participants use the Great Invocation in a spirit of cooperation and selfless service to stimulate and increase the flow of light and goodwill worldwide. Through its repeated use, a dual integration-fusion process blends personality and soul within an individual, group, or nation while synthesizing each within the greater whole. It expresses certain central truths: that an essential Intelligence is guiding the universe, working out Its Purpose (*the Great Good*) through Love, which motivates and implements the divine Plan (*the Good*) through humanity, which Christ most fully embodied.

Another aspect of the potency of this group work rests in the fact that the invocation should be used and sounded as *voiced demands* and *affirmed beliefs*. The Ancient Wisdom tells us that this invocation breaks the impasse between good and evil, light and dark, and between a return to the materialistic past and a more divine future. Still, the guarantee of a better tomorrow must come from a sensed vision that dawns upon the minds of human beings throughout the world so that they will choose to allow even more light and love into their minds, transforming their thoughts and actions. To this, each of us can add our efforts in just a few minutes each day.

The Great Invocation

From the point of Light within the Mind of God
Let light stream forth into human minds.
Let Light descend on Earth.
From the Point of Love within the Heart of God
Let love stream forth into human hearts.
May the Coming One return to Earth.
From the center where the Will of God is known
Let purpose guide all little human wills –
The purpose which the Masters know and serve.
From the center which we call the human race
Let the Plan of Love and Light work out
And may it seal the door where evil dwells.
Let Light and Love and Power restore the Plan on Earth.

OM OM OM

*A video visual is also available:
https://www.youtube.com/watch?v=-eSFGKhxRiM&t=29s

TAISHA LALANAI RUCKER is an attorney, educator, and founder of One Humanity, a not-for-profit organization providing inspiration, education, and training to help others learn to serve the common good.